Penguin Handbooks
Favourite Food

Josceline Dimbleby made her name as an imaginative cookery writer
with *A Taste of Dreams*. This was followed by *Party Pieces*, a booklet
for the Victoria and Albert Museum's Silver Jubilee exhibition of
Young British Craftsmen, and by a personal and highly successful
series of cookery books for Sainsbury's. In 1979 she won the André
Simon Memorial Fund Book Award for her *Book of Puddings,
Desserts and Savouries*, which is also published as a Penguin
Handbook. She has contributed to a number of newspapers and
magazines and has appeared on both television and radio. She is
now Cookery Editor of the *Sunday Telegraph*.

She lives in London and Devon with her husband, the broadcaster
David Dimbleby, and their three children.

Josceline Dimbleby
Favourite Food

Penguin Books

For my children, Liza, Henry and Kate,
who taste and tell.

Penguin Books Ltd, Harmondsworth, Middlesex, England
Viking Penguin Inc., 40 West 23rd Street, New York, New York 10010, U.S.A.
Penguin Books Australia Ltd, Ringwood, Victoria, Australia
Penguin Books Canada Ltd, 2801 John Street, Markham, Ontario, Canada L3R 1B4
Penguin Books (N.Z.) Ltd, 182–190 Wairau Road, Auckland 10, New Zealand

First published by Allen Lane 1983
Published in Penguin Books 1984

Filmset, printed and bound in Great Britain by
Hazell Watson & Viney Limited,
Member of the BPCC Group,
Aylesbury, Bucks
Set in VIP Times

Contents

Introduction

In 1975 I bought a loose-leaf notebook and began writing down my first recipes. Since getting married my enthusiasm for inventive cookery had grown in leaps and bounds, and although my life was now dominated by the demands of two little children and a baby I found that creativity in the kitchen was still possible. It gave me great satisfaction and a feeling of some independence. I had begun singing lessons again once a week but it was hard to practise and when I did my son would come into the room with his fingers in his ears and an expression of agony on his face. I noticed that even during my singing lessons the conversation would often turn to food; love of food and music often seem to go together.

I tried out my gastronomic ideas on people who came to dinner, and it was these enthusiastic friends who persuaded me that I should write some of the recipes down so that they could make them too. But it was my sister-in-law, with the positive attitude of a professional journalist, who finally encouraged me to approach a publisher.

It was all very satisfying, an enjoyable project which fitted in with family life. I never dreamed that I would write more books; even during my years at music college I had never had the confidence to picture myself as a real professional in any field. Yet once my book was out and I received my first treasured letters from people who had actually cooked my food, and liked it, it seemed perfectly natural that I should begin to write another book. Even now, several cooking years and books later, I still consider myself an enthusiastic amateur cook who happens to have some inspiring ideas which I want to impart. It is like the urge one has to tell people when one has enjoyed a book, a play or even a holiday very much; because I so enjoy food and the discovery of new tastes I long to tell other people about it, in the hope that I can persuade them to share my enthusiasm.

I think enthusiasm is really the subject of this book. I have written books on various kinds of cooking and food for different occasions, but I felt it was time now for a book of favourites. However, they are by no means all old favourites; what excites me is moving on and finding more good tastes, so there are a lot of new favourites too which emerged while I wrote the book.

A collection of recipes like this obviously reflects my own way of life, so there are plenty of recipes which will do for family meals. You may have children who profess to like only fish fingers or roast chicken – all I can say is, persevere with your cooking and, while not forcing them to eat up what you produce, always try to make them taste it. I have found that a morsel of good flavour tried by the most culinarily reluctant child can lead to a completely new attitude to certain food. Everyone, myself included, gets bogged down at some point by everyday cooking for the family, but I am convinced that the way to make it more enjoyable is through variety. So don't let your children's limited tastes dominate you; however much they may beg for chicken and peas, their palates are never too young to be educated, and it will bring them both interest and pleasure very soon.

The most satisfying hours of cooking for me are definitely for special occasions. If I have enough time, an amusing event with appreciative guests to prepare for and, best of all, an undisturbed kitchen in which I can listen to a complete opera while I cook, I can be very happy. An afternoon such as this has inspired many of the more glamorous recipes in this book, as has the kind of dazzling summer day when I have longed to be out in my garden instead of at the stove, and consequently have produced something quick, refreshing and pretty; a complement to the weather.

The varieties of climate, situation and mood in our lives gives us a need for different kinds of food and gives me, at any rate, inspiration to keep changing. I also rely heavily on travel to broaden my gastronomic horizons and show me that unusual methods of cookery can reveal endless mouth-watering possibilities.

I travelled throughout my childhood and am still lucky enough to travel often. My journeys are certainly reflected in many of my recipes and sometimes I feel that with me both travel and food are almost an addiction. As soon as I began to earn any money I put some away in what I think of as a 'travelling fund' to ensure that whatever happens at any time there will still be the possibility of at least one more journey of adventure. As for cooking itself, although a break from the responsibilities of my kitchen is always the most relaxing treat, I still find that after even a week away from the stove I am quite glad to get back to it, my energy recharged and my imagination refreshed.

I recently had to undergo a signing session for my latest cookery book. Unless you are an extraordinarily bold person this can be an embarrassing experience. I sat there feeling nervous and foolish at a little plastic desk covered with copies of my book. For some time nothing happened and people walked quickly past trying not to catch my eye. Then the photographer from the local paper arrived and made me feel even more ridiculous by getting me to pose for him holding up a saucepan and frying pan piled with my cookery books on either side of my scarlet, blushing face. But eventually all sorts of nice people came up and I even began to enjoy it, enough to be able to face with confidence the ones who glanced at my book with a bored look saying that they had far too many cookery books at home already. 'Ah,' I said, 'but I promise you, none of the recipes in any of those books will be quite like these.'

Starters, Salads
and Accompaniments

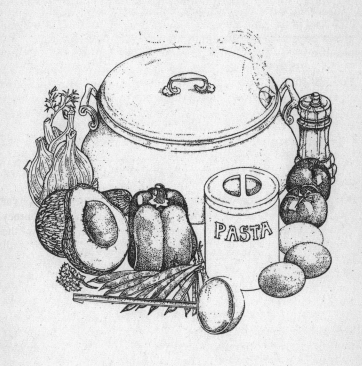

Almond and Chive Soup (for 4)

Here is a creamy but tangy cold soup with a delicious crunch of toasted almonds. It is perfect for hot summer days and, since it needs no cooking, leaves you plenty of time for sunbathing!

2–3 oz (50–75 g) flaked almonds
1 family size carton plain yogurt
½ pint (300 ml) single cream
a little milk

salt, black pepper
2–3 teaspoons fresh or dried chives, chopped

Spread the almonds on a baking sheet and put into a high oven for only a few minutes until toasted golden brown. Watch carefully so that they don't burn. Then stir the yogurt and the single cream together thoroughly until very smooth, and add just enough milk to give the consistency of a medium thick soup. Season to taste with salt and black pepper and chill well in the fridge. Shortly before serving add the finely chopped chives, followed by the toasted almonds.

Broad Bean and Apple Soup (for 4–5)

This creamy soup has a subtle flavour which people find hard to identify but always enjoy. Serve it either hot or chilled according to the weather.

2 oz (50 g) butter or margarine
1 large cooking apple
8 oz (225 g) podded broad beans, fresh or frozen
1 small onion, peeled and sliced
1 level teaspoon mixed spice
2 rounded tablespoons plain flour

1½ pints (900 ml) water
2 teaspoons French mustard
½ pint (300 ml) single cream
salt, black pepper
2–3 teaspoons lemon juice
handful fresh chives or parsley, finely chopped

Melt the butter in a fairly large, heavy saucepan. Peel and core the apple, cut into rough chunks and stir into the butter. Add the broad beans, the sliced onion and the spice. Stir around and then stir in the flour. Add the water and bring to the boil, stirring all the time, then cover the pan and simmer gently for 10–15 minutes or until the apples are mushy. Stir in the mustard and allow to cool for a bit. Then liquidize until very smooth. Pour back into the saucepan, add the single cream and re-heat gently. Season to taste with salt and black pepper and stir in the lemon juice. Before serving sprinkle with chopped chives.

Carrot and Orange Soup (for 6)

Served chilled and sprinkled with fresh chives, this is a most refreshing soup. Served hot with croûtons of fried bread it takes on a different character and is rich and sustaining.

1½ lb (675 g) carrots
2–3 large cloves garlic, peeled
juice of 1 lemon
grated rind of 1 orange
1 pint (600 ml) water

¼–½ whole nutmeg, grated
juice of 3 oranges
½ pint (300 ml) single cream
salt, black pepper

Wash and scrape the carrots and cut up roughly. Put into a saucepan with the garlic, lemon juice, grated orange rind and water. Cover the pan, bring to the boil and simmer for about 30 minutes until the carrots are soft. Add the nutmeg and leave to cool a little. Then add the orange juice and liquidize until smooth. Stir in the single cream and season to taste with salt and black pepper. Either re-heat or serve chilled. If when chilled it seems too thick, stir in some milk.

Swede and Cranberry Soup (for 6)

This beautifully pink soup is good for a guessing game – 'Tomato?' people ask. 'Or beetroot?' But they know from the refreshingly unusual taste, both slightly sweet and sharp, that it is in fact neither of these. You can serve the soup either hot or cold, with some nutty brown bread.

1 lb (450 g) swede
2½ pints (1·4 litres) water
6 whole cloves garlic, peeled
1 tablespoon caster sugar

6 oz (175 g) fresh cranberries
salt, black pepper
½ pint (300 ml) soured cream

Peel the swede, cut up roughly and put into a saucepan with the water, garlic and caster sugar. Cover the pan, bring to the boil, and then simmer for about 30 minutes until the swede is completely soft. Then add the cranberries, cover the pan and continue to cook for 10 minutes. Let the soup cool, then whizz up in a liquidizer or food processor until smooth. Sieve the soup back into a saucepan to remove all traces of cranberry pips and skin, and season to taste with salt and black pepper. Re-heat the soup and serve in individual soup bowls with a dollop of soured cream in the centre of each.

Cucumber and Green Peppercorns in Aspic (for 6)

These shining little moulds are a first course which I often resort to when I haven't much time. They are so easy to make yet always an awe-inspiring sight. If you are not familiar with the subtle aromatic flavour of green peppercorns, this is the time to discover it. For my moulds I use heart-shaped patty tins which give a particularly pretty result, but deep patty tins or cocotte dishes are fine. This decorative overture to the meal just tickles the appetite, which, if you want people to enjoy the main dish, is what a first course is for.

1 oz (25 g) aspic jelly powder	salt
just under 1 pint (600 ml) water	a few flat continental parsley leaves or
½ large cucumber	tiny mint leaves
1 heaped teaspoon green peppercorns	1 carton soured cream
(available in jars)	4 tablespoons plain yogurt
1 tablespoon lemon juice	

Put the aspic powder and the water in a saucepan and bring to the boil, stirring until dissolved. Remove from the heat. Peel the cucumber, dice it into small cubes and add it to the hot aspic liquid together with the green peppercorns. Stir in the lemon juice and season with a little salt if necessary. Strain the liquid into another saucepan or jug. Lay a parsley leaf or two on the bottom of each mould. Then divide the cucumber and peppercorns evenly between 6 moulds and pour the aspic liquid over them up to the top. Cool and then put in the fridge to set.

Shortly before serving, mix the soured cream and yogurt together and spoon a thin layer over 6 flat individual plates. Then dip the moulds briefly into hot water and shake to turn out. Place them carefully on each plate in the centre of the sauce. Refrigerate again until the last moment.

Spinach and Egg Cocottes (for 4)

This is an extremely decorative dish and makes a perfect first course for a dinner party. It is easy to do and can be made well ahead. Stripes of spinach and egg are held together with lemon aspic and garnished with golden pieces of grated carrot in aspic. If you have no little moulds you can of course use one large one.

1 lb (450 g) spinach	3 eggs, boiled until the yolks are just
1 pint (600 ml) water	set, about 5 minutes
1 oz (25 g) aspic jelly powder	salt, pepper
juice of ½ lemon	1 carrot, peeled and coarsely grated

Pick the stalks from the spinach and boil the leaves in a little salted water for 3–5 minutes until soft. Drain well and chop up finely. Bring the water to the boil and dissolve the aspic jelly powder in it. Add the lemon juice to the dissolved aspic and leave to cool slightly. Peel and roughly chop the boiled eggs and sprinkle with a little salt and pepper. Spoon a little aspic on to the bottom of 8 cocotte dishes or deep patty tins. Put in half the chopped spinach, then the egg, and top with the remaining spinach. Spoon aspic into the moulds, letting them absorb it and adding a little more. Strain the remaining aspic into a wide, shallow tin and stir in the grated carrot. Leave to cool and then chill both the spinach moulds and the carrot aspic in the fridge.

When chilled dip the moulds briefly in hot water and shake out. Arrange on a serving dish. Dip the cake tin of carrot and aspic briefly in hot water, turn out and cut into little pieces. Use these to decorate all round the spinach moulds. Keep in the fridge until ready to eat.

Water Lily Timbale (for 8)

I have two friends who make this dish over and over again since they had it with me the first time, because, they say, it is such a continual success. It really is a wonderfully decorative and appetizing dish, always impressive for a cold lunch party or as a first course at a dinner party. A creamy purée of carrots sandwiches a centre of avocado and the whole is wrapped in tender leaves of spinach. The water lily effect is made by edging the timbale with a circular fan of chicory leaves and putting a little coarsely grated carrot in the centre.

1 lb (450 g) spinach
2 lb (900 g) carrots
4–5 whole unpeeled cloves garlic
1 oz (25 g) powdered gelatine
4 tablespoons lemon juice
6 tablespoons olive oil
2–3 teaspoons Dijon mustard

2 teaspoons caster sugar
¼ whole nutmeg, grated
salt, black pepper
2 avocados
a little coarsely grated raw carrot
1–2 chicory heads

Wash and take the stalks off the spinach and boil the whole leaves in salted water just for a moment until they become limp. Peel and roughly slice the carrots and boil with the unpeeled cloves of garlic until well cooked. While they are boiling, well oil a 9–10 inch (23–25 cm) china flan dish or other round shallow bowl. Line with three-quarters of the spinach leaves, laying them on top of each other and bringing them up and a little over the sides of the dish. Dissolve the gelatine in a little water over a gentle heat. Purée the boiled carrots in a liquidizer or food processor with the cloves of garlic which you pop out of their skins, the dissolved gelatine, the lemon juice, olive oil, mustard, sugar, and nutmeg, and salt and black pepper to taste.

Allow the purée to cool a little and then spoon half of it into the spinach case.

Cut the avocados in half, carefully peel off the skin and slice thinly across. Lay the slices on top of the carrot. Spoon on the remaining carrot purée and smooth the top. Bring any overlapping spinach leaves in over the filling and lay the remaining leaves on top of the carrot. Brush with a little oil, cover with cling film, and refrigerate for several hours or overnight.

Turn out on to a serving dish, loosening the edges carefully with a knife if necessary. Brush the top again with oil to make it really shiny and put the grated carrot in the centre. Separate the chicory leaves and arrange them fanning outwards round the spinach timbale.

Cheese and Courgette Terrine
en Croûte (for 6–8)

A tasty combination of cheeses holding together a centre of baby courgettes and wrapped in a crust of rich pastry. This can be either part of a cold meal with salad or, sliced neatly, an interesting first course, served either cold or lukewarm.

For the pastry
6 oz (175 g) strong plain flour
good pinch salt
4 oz (100 g) butter
1 egg, whisked
1 tablespoon cold water

For the filling
6–7 baby courgettes, approx. 6 oz
  (175 g)

8 oz (225 g) curd cheese
2 tablespoons single cream or top of
  the milk
4 oz (100 g) coarsely grated Gruyère
  or Emmenthal cheese
¼–½ teaspoon cayenne pepper
a little grated nutmeg
salt

To make the pastry, sift the flour and salt into a bowl and rub in the butter with your fingertips until the mixture resembles breadcrumbs. Using a knife, mix in the whisked egg and the cold water until the pastry starts to stick together. Then gather into a ball and leave in the fridge while you prepare the filling.

Top and tail the courgettes. Mix the curd cheese in a bowl with the cream. Stir in the grated Gruyère or Emmenthal and season with cayenne pepper, grated nutmeg and a little salt. Butter a small bread tin about 1 pint (600 ml) capacity. Cut off three-quarters of the pastry and roll out on to a floured surface into a piece big enough to line the tin and slightly overlap the edges. Cut the uneven overlapping edges off to leave about ¾ inch (1·5 cm) all round. Add the pastry scraps to the remaining quarter of pastry. Heat the oven to Gas 5/375°F/190°C.

Spread half the cheese mixture on the bottom of the pastry-lined tin and lay the whole courgettes over the cheese, cutting if necessary to fit closely. Then spread the remaining cheese mixture on top. Bring the overlapping pieces of pastry in over the cheese. Roll out the remaining pastry into a rectangle big enough to form a lid. Moisten the underside edges, lay on top of the tin, and press down at the sides; cut off the edges neatly, roll out the scraps and use for decoration. Pierce two holes in the pastry and brush with a little milk. Cook in the centre of the oven for 30–40 minutes until golden brown. Leave to cool in the tin and then turn out. To serve, cut across in slices using a sharp knife. If using as a first course, lay each slice on an individual serving dish garnished with lettuce or watercress.

Tomato Egg Cups (for 4)

A very decorative cold first course. These are large tomatoes stuffed with soft poached egg under a creamy tomato, dill and garlic sauce into which the yolk mingles beautifully as you break it. In spite of the quantity of garlic this sauce has a mild, subtle flavour.

4–5 large cloves garlic	3 fl oz (80 ml) whipping cream
2 very large firm tomatoes	salt
1 level teaspoon caster sugar	cayenne pepper
squeeze lemon juice	a few crisp lettuce leaves or
2–3 teaspoons fresh or dried dill	watercress to garnish
4 eggs	

Boil the unpeeled cloves of garlic in some water until soft – about 10–15 minutes. Pour boiling water over the tomatoes, skin them and cut them in half. Carefully scoop out the flesh – I do it with a curved grapefruit knife. Put the tomato shells either on one large or on individual serving plates. Pop the cloves of garlic out of their skins into a liquidizer, add the scooped-out tomato flesh, the caster sugar and the lemon juice. Whizz up until very smooth. Then stir in the chopped dill and leave in the fridge to get cold.

Meanwhile, poach the eggs lightly in oiled poachers for 4–5 minutes so that the yolks will still be runny. Turn the eggs out into the tomato shells. When the tomato mixture is cold whip the cream until stiff and fold the tomato mixture into it. Season with salt and cayenne pepper to taste, remembering that it must be well seasoned to flavour the egg and tomato shell as well.

If you don't want to eat at once, leave the creamy sauce in the fridge, but not the tomatoes and eggs as they should not be too cold. Then before serving spoon the sauce over the top and sprinkle each tomato with a pinch of cayenne pepper. Garnish with lettuce or watercress round the tomatoes.

Wholewheat Pasta Salad with Anchovies and Fennel (for 4)

Wholewheat macaroni gives this salad a nutty taste which combines well with the very delicate flavour of anchovies and root fennel. It is quite a filling salad, which makes it a perfect cold lunch, accompanied by green salad and perhaps a tomato salad too. It also goes well with simple cold chicken or ham.

4 oz (100 g) wholewheat macaroni
1 small piece bulb fennel, thinly sliced
½ bunch parsley or fresh mint leaves, finely chopped

1 can anchovy fillets
black pepper
French dressing with added mustard and 1 small clove crushed garlic

Boil the macaroni in salted water until cooked. Drain, rinse thoroughly in cold water and leave to cool. Put the cold pasta into a salad bowl or dish with the sliced fennel and chopped parsley. Empty the oil from the can of anchovies into the salad, chop the anchovies into very small pieces and add them too. Season with plenty of black pepper. Before serving mix in the French dressing thoroughly and sprinkle a little extra chopped parsley on top.

Potato Dumplings with Cheese and Garlic in Fresh Tomato Sauce (for 4-6)

My elder daughter has become a vegetarian so she is particularly pleased when we have this dish as a main course for supper, accompanied by a crisp green salad. Alternatively it can be a side dish as part of a more substantial meal.

1½–2 lb (675–900 g) potatoes
1–2 oz (25–50 g) butter
milk
4 oz (100 g) plain flour
2 cloves garlic, crushed
6 oz (175 g) grated cheese
2 eggs, beaten
salt, black pepper

For the sauce
1 lb (450 g) squashy tomatoes
juice of 1 lemon
2–3 oz (50–75 g) butter
2 heaped teaspoons oregano
salt, black pepper
a little grated cheese

Peel and boil the potatoes and drain well. Mash smoothly with the butter and a little milk. Mix in the flour, the crushed garlic, the grated cheese and the beaten eggs, and season with salt and black pepper. Leave to cool.

Meanwhile, make the sauce. Pour boiling water over the tomatoes and skin them. Chop up roughly and cook very gently in a pan with the lemon juice, butter and oregano, stirring around until they have disintegrated into a sauce. Season with salt and black pepper and keep warm.

Now, using well-floured hands, take up bits of the potato mixture and form ping-pong sized balls. Bring a large pan of water to the boil. Drop in the dumplings and boil for about 5 minutes – they will rise to the top when cooked. Take out carefully with a slotted spoon and put on to a warm serving plate. Pour the tomato sauce over them, sprinkle with a little grated cheese and serve.

Basmati Rice with Whole Spices (for 5–6)

Basmati rice is smaller than ordinary long grain rice and has a delicious nutty flavour which I feel is far superior to other rice. However, it must be cooked perfectly. I find that this recipe is best and the delicately aromatic rice goes well with endless dishes. Whenever I serve basmati rice cooked in this way, people invariably comment that it is the best rice they have ever eaten.

8 oz (225 g) basmati rice	2–3 inches (5–7·5 cm) cinnamon sticks
1 tablespoon sunflower oil	a little more than ½ pint (300 ml)
1 oz (15 g) butter	water
5–8 whole cardamom pods	1 level teaspoon salt

Put the rice into a sieve and wash through well with cold water. Then put into a bowl with 1 pint (600 ml) salted water and soak for 30 minutes. Drain. Heat the oil and butter in a saucepan, add the cardamom pods and cinnamon sticks and stir around for a moment, then add the drained rice. Pour in the water and stir in the salt. Bring to the boil, cover tightly and reduce the heat to as low as possible for 12–15 minutes only until the rice is tender but still has a very slight bite to it. Using a fork, turn out on to a warm serving dish.

Aubergines with Ladies' Fingers (for 6–8)

This is a most versatile dish. It is similar to ratatouille and makes an excellent first course, served cold. You can also have it as a hot vegetable main course served with rice or simply as an accompaniment to roast lamb, pork or chicken. Ladies' fingers, otherwise known as okra or bindhi, are little pointed green vegetables found in many markets and greengrocers nowadays, and in most Indian grocery shops. They add a good contrasting texture to this dish.

1–1¼ lb (450–550 g) aubergines
6 oz (175 g) fresh ladies' fingers
olive or sunflower oil
2 largish onions, sliced
2 large cooking tomatoes, sliced
2 cloves garlic, finely chopped
2 teaspoons paprika

1 teaspoon cinnamon
1 tablespoon tomato paste
¼ pint (150 ml) water
salt
¼–½ teaspoon chilli powder
juice of 1 lemon

Cut the aubergines into largish chunks, rub all over with salt and leave in a colander for at least 30 minutes. (This drains the bitter juices away and stops them absorbing huge quantities of oil during cooking.) Cut the ends off the ladies' fingers and fry in a little oil just until browned. Transfer to a casserole. Put the sliced onion and tomatoes into the frying pan, adding more oil if necessary, until the onions begin to soften. Add to the ladies' fingers. Then rinse and drain the aubergine pieces and fry in oil for a moment each side just to brown. Add to the casserole. Lastly, quickly fry the chopped garlic, the paprika and the cinnamon for a moment and add. Heat the oven to Gas 4/350°F/180°C.

Put the tomato paste in a mixing jug, add the water, and season with a little salt and chilli powder. Add the lemon juice and pour the mixture over the vegetables. Cover the dish and cook in the oven for about 30 minutes or until all the vegetables are soft. Serve hot or cold.

Quince and Pimento Ratatouille (for 4)

This is a hot ratatouille to serve with sausages, pork chops, roast pork, gammon or duck. Use cooking apples if you have no quinces, though it won't have quite the same flavour.

1 large green pepper
1 large red pepper
1 large onion
2–3 tablespoons olive or sunflower oil
2 large tomatoes, peeled and chopped
2–3 cloves garlic, chopped

1 large quince
2 teaspoons sugar
salt, black pepper
finely chopped spring onions
  (optional)

Remove the seeds from the peppers and slice. Peel and slice the onion. Heat the oil in a large deep pan or iron casserole dish. Put in the peppers, the onion and the chopped tomatoes. Cook over a gentle heat, stirring around, until beginning to soften. Add the garlic. Peel and core the quinces, slice up thinly and add to the pan. Stir in the sugar. Cover with foil or a lid and continue cooking over a gentle heat for about 10 minutes until the quince is soft. Season with salt and black pepper.

I often sprinkle finely chopped spring onion over ratatouille just before serving. It adds a good contrast of flavour and texture.

Tomatoes Stuffed with Pork and Cheese

(for 4)

Some recipes for stuffed tomatoes give a rather stodgy filling including breadcrumbs or rice. This is not one of them. These can be served either hot or cold as a first course or as the main course of a light meal accompanied by rice and a green salad. They really are delicious!

4 very large tomatoes
2 tablespoons olive oil
2 cloves garlic, finely chopped
1 sprig rosemary, finely chopped
1 level tablespoon caster sugar

salt, black pepper
8 oz (225 g) minced pork
2 oz (50 g) Gruyère, Emmenthal or
  Jarlsberg cheese, grated
5–6 fresh basil leaves, roughly chopped

Slice the tops off the tomatoes and scoop out all the seeds and most of the flesh. Chop the flesh up into small pieces. Salt the insides of the tomatoes and lay upside down in a colander to drain away the liquid.

In a large frying pan heat 1 tablespoon of olive oil and add the tomato pulp and chopped flesh. Add the chopped garlic and rosemary. Bubble over a high heat, stirring around all the time for 4–5 minutes until reduced and fairly thick. Stir in the caster sugar and bubble for a minute more. Remove from the heat and season well with salt and black pepper. Spoon the sauce into a bowl and put on one side.

Heat another tablespoon of oil in the frying pan. Season the meat with salt and pepper and fry over a high heat, stirring round with a wooden spoon, for about 5 minutes until well browned and separated. Stir into the tomato sauce. Then add the grated cheese and chopped basil leaves.

Rinse the salt from the tomato shells and dry with absorbent paper. Heat the oven to Gas 4/350°F/180°C. Place the tomato shells in an open ovenproof dish, spoon in the meat mixture, and then replace the cut-off tops of the tomatoes. Brush the tomatoes all over with oil and cook in the centre of the oven for 20–30 minutes until the tomatoes are soft.

Tomatoes Stuffed with Aubergine Cream and Kiwi Fruit (for 8)

This is a spectacular and mouth-watering first course. The combination of colours makes it look like a work of art and I always try to use plates with plenty of green in them to enhance this effect.

2 large aubergines, 1¼–1½ lb (550–675 g)	salt, black pepper
juice of ½ lemon	2 tablespoons olive oil
8 very large firm red tomatoes	½ pint (300 ml) double cream
2 teaspoons caster sugar	2–3 pinches cayenne pepper
	6 kiwi fruit

Put the aubergines, unpeeled, under a very hot grill, turning now and then until blackened and really burnt on all sides (it does not matter if they split open) – this usually takes 20–30 minutes. Run cold water over the aubergines just to make them cool enough to handle, and then scoop out the flesh into a sieve. Press out any liquid with a wooden spoon and put into a liquidizer or food processor with the lemon juice. Whizz to a purée and leave on one side.

Now cut off the very top of each tomato. Carefully scoop out the insides with a teaspoon (leaving a casing of firm flesh), and put into a saucepan together with the tops. Add the caster sugar and season with salt. Cover the pan, bring to the boil and allow to simmer for 20–25 minutes. Meanwhile put the tomato shells, in two batches, in a bowl and pour boiling water over them, covering completely. Immediately pour off the boiling water and replace with cold. Take out the tomatoes and peel carefully – don't worry if you can't avoid any cracks or holes in the peeled shells, this won't matter. Leave on one side. When the tomato flesh is well cooked pour the juice through a sieve into a bowl, pressing as much flesh as possible through with a wooden spoon. Season with black pepper and stir in the olive oil. Spoon and spread the sauce thinly on to 8 individual serving plates.

Now whisk up the cream until thick, standing in soft peaks, but not too stiff. Stir the aubergine purée into it and season with the cayenne pepper and salt to taste. Peel 2 of the kiwi fruit, cut into small cubes, and stir these into the cream and aubergine mixture. Place the tomato shells in the centre of the sauce on the serving plates. Spoon the aubergine cream into each shell. Peel the remaining kiwi fruit and slice into thin rounds. Put one round on top of each filled tomato and arrange the other rounds on top of the sauce – 3–4 slices to each plate. Keep in a cool place or the fridge until ready to serve.

Minty Mushrooms

This dish is made in minutes and is always very popular as an accompaniment to either a hot or a cold meal. It is specially good with lamb.

¾ lb (340 g) small mushrooms, finely sliced, keeping their mushroom shape

2 small onions, very finely sliced in rings

large handful fresh mint leaves, roughly chopped

3 cloves garlic, crushed or finely chopped

5 tablespoons olive or sunflower oil

juice of 1 small lemon

white wine vinegar

salt, black pepper

Simply put all the prepared ingredients into a saucepan and season with a lot of freshly ground black pepper and a spoonful of salt. Mix up with a spoon, cover with a lid, and put the pan over a very low heat for not more than 4 or 5 minutes. Pour into a serving dish and either serve hot or cool in the fridge. If there are no potatoes, serve with brown bread so that greedy people can mop up any remaining delicious juices with it.

Leeks in Two Dressings (for 4–5)

Leeks are a great favourite of mine and this is a particularly good way of serving them cold. It will do either as a first course or as part of a salad meal with cold meats.

1 lb (450 g) thin leeks
1 tablespoon (15 ml) wine vinegar
5 tablespoons (75 ml) olive oil
salt, black pepper

1 bunch spring onions, finely chopped
5 fl oz (150 ml) double cream
2 tablespoons mayonnaise (a good commercial kind will do)

Cut the darker green ends off the leeks. Cut the leeks into 3 inch (7·5 cm) pieces and wash well. Plunge them into boiling salted water for 8–12 minutes, until they are tender when you insert a small sharp knife. Drain the leeks and arrange in one layer in a rather shallow serving dish. Mix together the vinegar and olive oil and season with salt and plenty of black pepper. Pour this dressing over the leeks while they are still hot. Sprinkle over the chopped spring onions, keeping back a spoonful for garnish, and leave to cool. Before serving, whisk up the double cream until thick and then thoroughly stir in the mayonnaise. Spoon this dressing all over the leeks and sprinkle over the reserved spring onions.

Leeks Cooked in Spiced Wine (for 4–5)

This is a good way of cooking leeks and one which will go well with roast meat. Alternatively I serve the dish cold with cold meats, especially ham, and good brown bread to mop up the juices.

4 large leeks
2 bay leaves
1 glass white wine

1 teaspoon pickling spice
2 tablespoons olive oil
salt, black pepper

Take the outside leaves from the leeks and wash well. Cut each leek into 2–3 inch pieces and put into a wide saucepan with the rest of the ingredients. Cover the dish and simmer very gently for 15–25 minutes or until the leeks are soft. Arrange the leeks on a serving dish and pour the juices and spices over the top. Cool and then chill in the fridge before serving with fresh brown bread which you can use to mop up the juices.

Courgette Fritters (for 6)

These crispy fritters are very popular towards the end of the summer when courgettes and small marrows are cheap. They can be either a dish on their own or an accompaniment to cold or hot meat or chicken.

1½ lb (675 g) courgettes or small marrows
2 cloves garlic
handful parsley
about 15 fresh mint leaves } very finely chopped

1 oz (25 g) grated Parmesan cheese
1 egg, lightly whisked
about 3 tablespoons plain flour
salt, black pepper
groundnut oil for deep frying

Peel the courgettes and grate the flesh into a bowl. Stir in the other ingredients, adding enough flour to bind the mixture fairly thickly. Heat plenty of oil in a large pan until smoking. Drop dessertspoons of the mixture into the oil and fry for 2–3 minutes until golden brown all over. Drain on absorbent paper.

Brussels Purée (for 4)

'What *can* this be?' friends ask, consuming it with enthusiasm. They guess at more exotic ingredients such as avocado and aubergine, but never do they suggest the modest Brussels sprout which is what the basis of this light and delicate purée really is. Very good with grilled meat or fish, served in conjunction with baby carrots.

8 oz (200 g) prepared Brussels sprouts, fresh or frozen
3 oz (75 g) crustless white bread
2 tablespoons (30 ml) lemon juice
2 oz (50 g) unsalted butter (at room temperature)

¼ whole nutmeg, grated
salt
2–3 pinches cayenne pepper
½ tablespoon olive oil
½ teaspoon paprika
chopped parsley to garnish

Cook the prepared sprouts in boiling salted water for 5–10 minutes until just tender but still bright green. Drain. Dip the bread into hot water and squeeze out. Put the sprouts, bread, lemon juice and butter into a food processor or liquidizer and whizz all together until very smooth. Season to taste with grated nutmeg, salt and cayenne pepper.

Spoon into a pretty serving dish. Just before serving mix the olive oil and paprika together in a cup, dribble over the purée, and sprinkle with a little chopped parsley.

French Bean and Red Pepper Salad (for 4)

This excellent salad is a mixture of blanched beans and rings of pepper dotted with skinless broad beans. The contrast of brilliant red and bright green makes it very eye-catching and it goes perfectly with cold meat.

12 oz (350 g) French beans
2 medium red peppers
6 oz (175 g) frozen broad beans

vinaigrette dressing with ½ clove garlic, crushed

Top and tail the French beans, and if very long cut into 3 inch (7 cm) lengths. Slice the red peppers crossways into thin rings. Plunge both vegetables into boiling salted water for 4 minutes. Drain, rinse well with cold water and leave to cool. Put the frozen broad beans in a bowl and pour boiling water over them. Leave for a minute and then pop them out of their skins. Mix the cold French beans, the red peppers and the skinned broad beans together in a salad bowl. Dress with the vinaigrette dressing.

Green Pea Salad with Fresh Ginger and Olives (for 4)

This unusual salad, even with its rather exotic flavour, is extremely popular with both adults and children. It goes perfectly with cold chicken, duck or pork. It's a salad you can make well ahead.

12 oz (350 g) frozen peas
2 oz (50 g) stuffed green olives, roughly chopped
2 oz (50 g) candied peel

1 clove garlic, finely chopped
1 inch (2·5 cm) fresh root ginger, peeled and finely chopped
2 tablespoons lemon juice

7 tablespoons sunflower oil
1 heaped teaspoon paprika
a little salt

1 large bunch parsley or fresh mint,
  finely chopped

Put all the ingredients except the parsley into a saucepan. Put over a medium heat, cover the pan, and cook gently, stirring now and then, for 10 minutes. Remove from the heat and stir in the chopped parsley. Allow to become cold, then spoon into a bowl. If the salad sits in the bowl for a long time before serving, stir it around a bit at the last minute so that it is well coated and shiny with the juices.

Spinach Salad with Bacon (for 4–5)

This salad is well known and I love it. There is something wonderful about the mingling of hot crispy bacon and its juices with the vinaigrette dressing and slight bitterness of the raw spinach.

8 oz (225 g) fresh spinach, preferably
  small-leaved
8 oz (225 g) smoked streaky bacon

simple vinaigrette dressing
grated Parmesan cheese (optional)

Pick the stalks off the spinach. Put the leaves, cutting them up if they are large, into a salad bowl. Cut off the rind and slice the bacon into small pieces. Fry the bacon gently at first until the fat begins to run out, then at a higher heat until crispy. (If necessary, keep the bacon and its fat warm until you are ready to eat the salad.) Toss the vinaigrette dressing into the salad. Then toss in the bacon, sprinkle generously with grated Parmesan, and serve at once.

Broccoli and Avocado Salad (for 6)

I make this salad over and over again. It is very pretty and combines cooked and raw vegetables and contrasting textures.

12 oz (350 g) calabrese broccoli (this is the green kind with hardly any leaves, thickish stalks and large compact heads)
1 small red pepper, finely sliced in rings

lemon juice
1 large avocado
vinaigrette dressing with French mustard

Cut just the end of the stems off the broccoli. Steam or boil the broccoli for 4–5 minutes until bright green and still crunchy. Rinse under cold water and drain. Put into a salad bowl with the sliced pepper. Squeeze a little lemon juice into a mixing bowl. Cut the avocado in half, scoop out in chunks into the lemon juice and stir around. Add the broccoli, and before serving dress with the vinaigrette dressing.

Jerusalem Salad (for 4)

The mysterious flavour of Jerusalem artichokes makes a delicious alternative to a potato salad. Here they are subtly mixed with skinned broad beans and avocado. A perfect accompaniment to cold meat.

1 lb (450 g) Jerusalem artichokes
8 oz (225 g) packet frozen broad beans

1 avocado
bunch parsley, finely chopped
vinaigrette dressing

Scrub and peel the artichokes as well as you can (don't bother to do it too thoroughly as it takes too much time and a little peel tastes good), and slice thinly. Either steam or boil for only 3–4 minutes until very slightly cooked but still crunchy. Put into a salad bowl. Pour boiling water over the frozen broad beans and leave for a minute. Then pop the beans out of their skins into the salad bowl with the artichokes. Cut the avocado in half, carefully peel off the skin and slice the flesh thinly across in semi-circles. Add to the artichokes and beans and mix in the chopped parsley and some vinaigrette dressing.

Savoury Orange and Onion Salad (for 4–5)

The idea for this salad came from a 1920s recipe book, and it is excellent with duck (hot or cold), ham or pork.

3–4 medium onions
3 oranges
8–10 black olives
paprika

For the dressing
1 tablespoon orange flower water
2 teaspoons lemon juice
3 tablespoons sunflower oil
1–2 pinches cayenne pepper
salt

Peel and slice both the onions and the oranges very thinly in rounds, removing any pips and pith from the oranges. Arrange them in layers in a round dish. Dot the olives on top and sprinkle all over with paprika. Mix the dressing ingredients thoroughly together and pour them over the salad before serving.

Tomato and Kiwi Fruit Salad with Fresh Mint (for 4)

This savoury salad is actually made with fruit, tomatoes being officially a fruit and not a vegetable. It is the simplest mixture but the flavours are perfectly compatible and the combination looks beautiful too. Try it as a first course or between courses.

1 lb (450 g) tomatoes
4–5 kiwi fruit
handful fresh mint leaves, chopped
vinaigrette dressing

Slice the tomatoes across in rounds and put into a glass bowl. Peel the kiwi fruit carefully, slice thinly across in rounds and mix with the tomatoes. Gently mix in the chopped mint. Before serving dress with a simple vinaigrette dressing.

Cucumber with Cream Cheese Mayonnaise (for 4)

Cucumber salads are always refreshing. Here the cucumber is mixed with chopped onion and mint and wrapped in a light mayonnaise made with cream cheese instead of egg. It makes a good first course.

4 oz (100 g) cream cheese	½ large cucumber, peeled and cut
3 tablespoons lemon juice	into cubes
4 tablespoons olive oil	1 small onion, finely chopped
4 tablespoons sunflower oil	1 heaped teaspoon fresh mint or
salt, black pepper	parsley, finely chopped

Put the cream cheese in a liquidizer with 2 tablespoons of the lemon juice; add the olive and sunflower oil, two spoonfuls at a time, whizzing between each addition. Add the remaining tablespoon of lemon juice, and season to taste with salt and pepper. Turn into a mixing bowl. Shortly before eating, add the cucumber cubes, chopped onion and mint or parsley. Spoon into a pretty serving bowl and serve.

New Potato, Radish and Spring Onion Salad with Anchovy Dressing (for 4)

The strong tastes of the radishes, onions and anchovy complement each other to produce a delicious flavour, which is taken on by good waxy-textured new potatoes. This salad goes well with hot or cold meat and fish dishes.

12 oz (350 g) new potatoes, boiled	*For the dressing*
or steamed	1 can anchovies
bunch radishes	1 tablespoon lemon juice
bunch spring onions	1 small clove garlic, peeled
	4 tablespoons sunflower oil
	black pepper

When the potatoes are cold, slice them thinly crossways and put them in a salad bowl. Wash, top and tail the radishes and slice finely across. Cut the spring onions into small pieces. Mix all together with the potatoes in the bowl. Put the anchovies and their oil in a liquidizer with the lemon juice and garlic and give a whizz. Then, still whizzing, add the oil a little at a time until you have a smooth dressing. Season with black pepper. If it should curdle, whizz in 1 tablespoon of warm water. Dress the salad thoroughly with the anchovy mixture.

Gruyère Salad Roulade (for 6–8)

This makes a most impressive first course but it is not difficult to achieve. It is substantial enough for a light cold lunch in the summer. You can of course experiment with different fillings according to what is in season or what you like.

grated Parmesan cheese
2 oz (50 g) fresh white breadcrumbs
6 oz (175 g) Gruyère cheese, finely grated
4 large eggs, separated
¼ pint (150 ml) single cream
salt, black pepper
cayenne pepper

2 tablespoons warm water
4–5 tablespoons mayonnaise
¼–½ crisp lettuce, shredded
2–3 tomatoes, finely sliced
1 oz (25 g) mushrooms, finely sliced
1 tablespoon fresh basil or mint leaves, chopped
watercress to garnish

Line a large Swiss roll tin with a piece of greased greaseproof paper and sprinkle with a little grated Parmesan. Mix the breadcrumbs and grated Gruyère cheese together in a mixing bowl. Heat the oven to Gas 6/400°F/200°C. Add the yolks of the eggs and the cream to the breadcrumbs and grated cheese and mix in. Season with salt and 2–3 pinches of cayenne pepper. Stir in the warm water to soften the mixture. Add a pinch of salt to the egg whites and whisk until they stand in soft peaks, then fold gently into the cheese mixture with a metal spoon. Spoon the mixture into the prepared tin, and bake in the centre of the oven for 10–15 minutes until risen and firm to a light touch. Remove and cool slightly – it will shrink a little but don't worry. Lay a damp tea cloth over the top and leave until cold. Then loosen the edges with a sharp knife.

Sprinkle a sheet of greaseproof paper all over with grated Parmesan and turn the cheese roulade out on to the paper. Spread generously with mayonnaise and then spread evenly with the shredded lettuce, the tomatoes, the mushrooms and the chopped basil or mint leaves. Season with a little salt and plenty of black pepper. Now roll up fairly loosely with the help of the greaseproof paper. Transfer carefully on to a bed of watercress on a serving dish. To serve, cut into slices across like a Swiss roll, using a very sharp knife.

Crumbled Cheese Salad (for 4)

It is easy to forget how enhanced cheese can be when coated with a good vinaigrette dressing. Even a spoonful of dressing put over a hunk of mousetrap at a hurried lunch of bread and cheese makes all the difference. In Greece the most everyday salad has in it pieces of their white Feta cheese. A similar salad made with crumbly English cheese is very good and the children love it, though they may pick out the olives.

1 small head Chinese leaves or cos
  lettuce, sliced
3 sticks celery, sliced thinly across
1 small onion, peeled and sliced finely
  in rings
3–4 tomatoes, sliced

2–3 oz (50–75 g) stoned black olives
1 tablespoon dried oregano
4 oz (100 g) Caerphilly, Wensleydale
  or other pale, crumbly cheese
French dressing with added mustard
  and garlic

Mix all the salad ingredients together in a salad bowl. Crumble the cheese into small pieces and scatter on top. Before serving, dress with the French dressing.

The Maharajah's Salad (for 4)

This is a delicate salad of steamed chicken or turkey breast mixed with cucumber, with a subtle hint of India in the creamy sauce of aromatic coconut milk and yogurt. It makes a good main dish for a salad lunch during the summer. (Alternatively you can use cooked cold chicken you may have left over.)

½ pint (300 ml) milk
3 oz (75 g) desiccated coconut
2 cloves garlic, roughly chopped

¼ teaspoon chilli powder
3–4 crushed cardamom pods
salt

10–12 oz (275–350 g) chicken or turkey breast fillets, skinned
6 tablespoons plain yogurt

½ cucumber
finely chopped parsley to garnish

Bring the milk to the boil in a pan and add the coconut, garlic, chilli powder and cardamom pods and a sprinkling of salt. Boil for 3 minutes and then leave to get cold. Slice the chicken fillets into thin strips. Steam over boiling water either in a steamer or a large sieve suspended in a closed saucepan for 5–8 minutes until the chicken is white and cooked. Leave to cool.

When the coconut mixture is cold, press the liquid out through a sieve into a mixing bowl, pressing with a wooden spoon to get out every drop. Stir the yogurt into the coconut milk and test for seasoning. Spread the pieces of cold chicken in a rather shallow dish. Peel the cucumber, cut it in strips and then into smallish pieces, and arrange among the chicken. Shortly before serving, spoon the sauce over the dish and sprinkle on an extra pinch of chilli and a little finely chopped parsley.

Turkey Liver Salad (for 3–4)

Even people who profess to hate all liver wolf down these tender rose-tinged slices of turkey liver, enhanced by a slightly sweet soy dressing. Accompanied by tomato salad and fresh brown bread, this dish makes a perfect light meal. If you are in a hurry or even if not, the salad tastes excellent while the livers and beans are still slightly warm.

1 tablespoon sunflower oil
1 tablespoon lemon juice
8 oz (225 g) turkey livers
8 oz (225 g) French beans
4 spring onions

For the soy dressing
1 tablespoon red wine or cider vinegar
1 tablespoon soy sauce
2 teaspoon caster sugar
2 tablespoon sunflower oil
2–3 pinches sea salt
1–2 pinches cayenne pepper

Gently heat the oil and lemon juice in a frying pan. Lightly cook the whole turkey livers in the pan, turning once or twice for 6–8 minutes (they are ready when the blood has been running out for 2–3 minutes). Transfer to a cold plate and leave to cool. Meanwhile top and tail the beans and if very large cut into 2–3 inch (5–7·5 cm) lengths. Bring some salted water to the boil, put in the beans, and boil for just 3–4 minutes until bright green and still crunchy. Drain and rinse under cold water to cool.

When the livers are cold, slice thinly with a sharp knife crossways. Put the cold beans and liver in a salad bowl. Slice the spring onions into fine rings, using as much of the green stalk as possible. Mix the soy dressing ingredients together and leave for a little to let the sugar dissolve. Pour the dressing over the salad just before serving.

My Salad Niçoise (for 4–5)

There seem to be many varied recipes for Salad Niçoise. This is simply a personal version in which I incorporate the olives and anchovies with chopped walnuts in the dressing itself. It is a nutritious and substantial salad which acts ideally as a main course for a cold meal. I find it especially useful, as children nearly always like tuna fish, and so it is the kind of salad they will not spurn.

4 eggs	1 tin anchovies
1 green pepper	1 clove garlic
7 oz (200 g) can tuna	1 oz (25 g) walnuts
1 small onion, thinly sliced in rings	1 tablespoon wine vinegar
3–4 tomatoes, cut across in thin slices	2 tablespoons lemon juice
1 rounded teaspoon capers	5–6 tablespoons olive oil
1 oz (25 g) pitted olives	2–4 pinches cayenne pepper

Boil the eggs semi-hard and leave in cold water to cool. Put the green pepper under a hot grill, turning two or three times until it is blackened all over. Then rinse the pepper under cold water to cool, and peel off the skin. Cut in half, remove the stalk and seeds and slice into thin strips. Mix the tuna with the pepper, onion, tomatoes and capers in a wide, fairly shallow serving dish.

To make the dressing, chop the olives, anchovies, garlic and walnuts together as finely as possible. Put the mixture into a bowl and add the vinegar, lemon juice, oil and cayenne pepper (no salt – the anchovies will make it salty enough). Mix thoroughly together and then mix gently into the salad. Finally, shell the eggs, cut them in half lengthways and arrange evenly round the edge of the salad.

Smoky Aubergine Pâté (for 6–8)

This is a pale, mild and delicious pâté. It is particularly good spread on to pieces of celery and served as part of an hors d'oeuvre. It also makes a subtle first course served with toast.

2 large aubergines, approx. 1¼ lb
  (550 g)
3 large cloves garlic, unpeeled

1 tablespoon lemon juice
6 oz (175 g) full cream cheese
salt, black pepper

Put the whole aubergine under a very hot grill until black and blistered – 10–15 minutes on each side. Meanwhile, boil the cloves of garlic in a covered pan of water until they are soft. When the aubergines are blackened all over and soft inside, put them into cold water and remove the skin. Put the flesh into a sieve and squeeze out the water by pressing down with a wooden spoon, then transfer to a food processor or liquidizer with the lemon juice and the cloves of garlic, popped out of their skins. Whizz together. Add the cream cheese and whizz thoroughly until smooth. Finally, whizz in salt and black pepper to taste. Spoon the mixture into a serving bowl, cover with cling film, and chill in the fridge before serving.

Layered Paprika Pâté (for 6–8)

This is a pretty pâté which I often make for school holidays, as it is a great standby for cold lunches for an indeterminate number of people. It is also ideal for a buffet party. The tasty pork, wrapped neatly in bacon, sandwiches a softer chicken liver and paprika stripe in the centre. The pâté can be made well in advance and kept for at least a week in the fridge.

12 oz (350 g) streaky bacon, very
  thinly sliced with the rind cut off
1½ lb (675 g) fat belly of pork
6 oz (175 g) bacon scraps with the
  rind removed
3–5 teaspoons fresh marjoram or
  dried oregano

2 large cloves garlic, finely chopped
¼ whole nutmeg, grated
½ teaspoon peppercorns
salt, black pepper
12 oz (350 g) chicken livers
2 heaped teaspoons paprika
¼–½ teaspoon cayenne pepper

Line a 2½–3 pint (1·4–1·7 litre) ovenproof dish or tin neatly with strips of bacon – this will probably use up a little over half the bacon. Cut the skin off the belly of pork, and either by hand or in a food processor chop into small pieces together with the bacon scraps. Mix into the meat mixture the herbs, chopped garlic, nutmeg, whole peppercorns and plenty of salt and black pepper. Put a roasting pan of water in the oven and turn on to Gas 2/300°F/150°C.

Spoon half the meat mixture into the bacon-lined dish. Lay a layer of bacon strips on top. Now cut the chicken livers up finely and mix with the paprika, the cayenne and a good sprinkling of salt. Spoon this liver mixture into the dish and cover with another layer of bacon strips (remembering to reserve enough bacon for the top). Spoon the remaining meat mixture into the dish and cover with the rest of the bacon. Cover the dish with foil and put into the pan of water in the oven for 2½ hours. Allow to cool and then refrigerate until very cold.

To turn out, dip the dish briefly in very hot water and after a good shake or two the pâté should plop out on to a serving plate. I decorate the plate with parsley and thin half moon slices of a lemon and a small orange.

Liver and Apricot Terrine (for 6–8)

Terrines and pâtés are by no means always delicious. Such good things are packed into them and yet quite often what emerges has a bland and over-rich taste. Seasoning in a pâté is very important indeed. The sharp flavour of the dried apricots in this country terrine combines effectively with the aromatic mace, the juniper berries and the liqueur to give an interesting and appetizing flavour. Make the terrine at least a day before you plan to eat it.

1 lb (450 g) pig's liver
12 oz (350 g) belly of pork
4 oz (100 g) dried apricots
1–2 cloves garlic, crushed
10–15 juniper berries, roughly
  crushed
2 teaspoons ground mace (or nutmeg)

1 wineglass Cointreau (or brandy)
salt, black pepper
12 oz (350 g) smoked streaky bacon
  (if you have a friendly butcher ask
  him to cut the rind off the bacon
  and slice it as thinly as possible on
  his machine)

Chop the liver, the belly of pork and the dried apricots into very small pieces. Combine them in a bowl with the crushed garlic, juniper berries, mace, Cointreau, salt, black pepper and a few whole peppercorns if you like. Mix thoroughly together. Leave for an hour or more if possible so that the flavours blend together.

Line an earthenware bowl big enough to take this mixture with about half of the sliced streaky bacon. Spoon the liver mixture into the lined bowl and smooth down. Lay the remaining bacon neatly all over the top. Make a little pattern in the centre with anything you have – perhaps 2 or 3 bay leaves with some juniper berries and whole peppercorns. Cover the dish with foil and put it in a roasting pan of water in the centre of the oven at Gas 2/300°F/150°C for 1½–2 hours – it will be done when it starts to come away from the sides of the dish. When the juice and fat have started to cool put a weight on top of the foil and leave it in the fridge or a cool place until next day. Slice with a sharp knife and serve with a salad and some good brown bread.

Breast of Chicken, Veal and Lemon Terrine

This terrine has a stripe of marinated chicken livers in the centre while the pale meat either side has a refreshing lemon flavour. It's a good summer terrine to go with a salad.

8 oz (225 g) chicken livers	finely grated rind and juice of 1
white wine vinegar	lemon
8 oz (225 g) chicken breast fillets,	1 egg, whisked
skinned	1 clove garlic, crushed
8 oz (225 g) pie veal	chopped dill or tarragon
8 oz (225 g) pork fat	salt, black pepper

Chop the chicken livers finely, put into a small bowl, cover with vinegar and leave to marinate for 1–2 hours. Chop the chicken breast, the veal and the pork fat into small pieces and mix together in a bowl. Mix in the lemon rind and juice, the whisked egg, the crushed garlic and a good sprinkling of dill. Season well with salt and black pepper.

Spoon half the chicken and veal mixture into a 1½–2 pint (750 ml– 1 litre) ovenproof dish, then strain the chicken livers and spoon on top, followed by the remaining chicken and veal mixture. Fill a roasting pan with water and put it in the centre of the oven, and heat to Gas

3/325°F/170°C. Put the dish into the roasting pan and cook for 2 hours. Allow to cool and then chill in the fridge.

Chicken Liver Parfait (for 8)

This creamy smooth pâté is rich and deliciously mild. It makes an easy but luxurious first course. It's a natural for a food processor but if you don't have one you can press it through a sieve, though obviously this takes quite a lot longer.

8 oz (225 g) chicken livers
milk
6 oz (175 g) unsalted butter
salt, black pepper
1 tablespoon dry sherry

5 fl oz (150 ml) double cream
good pinch caster sugar
lettuce leaves, parsley or fennel, and
   thin half slices of lemon to garnish

Put the chicken livers in a bowl, cover with milk, and leave in the fridge to soak for several hours. Then drain. Heat the butter in a saucepan, add the drained chicken livers and season with salt and pepper. Cook very gently in the open pan, stirring around now and then for about 10 minutes. Leave until completely cold. Then whizz in a food processor until very smooth (don't leave the machine whizzing for too long or the butter will begin to melt and the mixture can curdle). Gradually whizz in the sherry. Transfer to a bowl.

Whisk the cream until thick but not stiff. Work the cream gently but thoroughly into the liver purée with a wooden spoon. Add the caster sugar and season to taste with salt and black pepper. Spoon into a small 1 pint (600 ml) round or oval dish and smooth the top. Chill well in the fridge. Then dip the dish in very hot water briefly, just until you can turn it out on to a serving dish, giving it a good shake. Immediately smooth all over with a knife. Garnish with some sprigs of parsley or fennel, lettuce leaves, and thin semi-circles of lemon all round the edge of the pâté. Serve with thin toast.

Yorkshire Pudding with Beer

This is a spectacular Yorkshire pudding. Since I had discovered the crisp lightness achieved by using beer instead of water or milk in batter for deep frying I experimented one day with Yorkshire pudding, using a mixture of milk and beer. As I opened the oven door we all shrieked at the sight inside because the pudding had risen so much that it had hit the oven roof. Not only does the yeast in beer cause this dramatic rising, it also makes a much crisper crust and a good flavour.

4 oz (100 g) plain flour
½ teaspoon salt
a little black pepper
1 large or 2 small eggs

4 fl oz (110 ml) beer
3–4 fl oz (80-110 ml) milk
1–2 tablespoons dripping

Sift the flour and salt, put into a liquidizer or food processor, and add the black pepper and the eggs. Whizz until smooth. With the motor running, add the beer and enough milk to make a smooth batter the consistency of thick cream, just dropping from a spoon. Let the batter stand at room temperature for 20 minutes or so. Heat the oven to Gas 5/375°F/190°C. Dot an ovenproof dish (I use a fairly large round china flan dish) with the fat and put just above the centre of the oven until smoking hot. Then pour in the batter and cook for 30–40 minutes until well risen and a rich brown.

Onion and Orange Chutney

A golden yellow translucent chutney which goes particularly well with game, pork or gammon. Because of its beautiful appearance it is perfect for presents and for school bazaars, etc.

1–2 fresh red chillies
6–8 cloves garlic
4–5 large onions
3 large oranges
8 oz (225 g) granulated sugar

10 whole cardamom pods, lightly
  crushed
1 teaspoon ground turmeric
½ pint (300 ml) white wine vinegar
¼ pint (150 ml) water

Cut open the chillies under running water and remove the seeds and stems. Peel the garlic. Chop the garlic and chillies together finely. Peel and chop the onions into small ½ inch (1 cm) pieces. Squeeze the juice out of all the oranges and put in a heavy saucepan. Scrape the pith out of the orange shells with a teaspoon, cut the peel into small pieces and add to the saucepan together with the chopped garlic and chillies and all the remaining ingredients. Stir together and bring to the boil, then simmer gently, uncovered, for about 1½ hours, stirring occasionally at first and more often as the mixture thickens. Cool and spoon into jars.

Cream Sauce with Green Peppercorns

(for 6)

This is an instant sauce to make and most useful for serving with grilled or fried fish, chicken or meat which might seem fairly dull or bland otherwise.

½ pint (300 ml) double or single
  cream
1 teaspoon green peppercorns,
  crushed

2 teaspoons white wine vinegar
salt

Gently heat the cream with the crushed peppercorns, but do not boil. Then gradually add the vinegar and stir over the heat, again not quite boiling, for a minute or two as the sauce thickens. Add salt to taste and pour into a sauce boat.

Herring Roe Cream
with Smoked Mackerel (for 6)

This is a delicate pâté or paste to eat with toast for a first course. It is extremely easy to make.

2 oz (50 g) butter
8 oz (225 g) soft herring roes
1 carton soured cream
¼ whole nutmeg, grated

cayenne pepper
salt
2 smoked mackerel fillets
finely chopped parsley to garnish

Melt the butter in a frying pan. Gently fry the herring roes for about 2 minutes until whitish and cooked. Put into a liquidizer or food processor with all the buttery juices and the soured cream. Whizz until smooth. Season with the grated nutmeg and cayenne pepper and salt to taste. Then skin the mackerel fillets and flake the flesh. Stir the flesh gently into the soft roe mixture, spoon into a serving bowl, sprinkle with a pinch of cayenne and make a narrow border round the edge with the chopped parsley. Chill for several hours in the fridge before eating.

Finnan Haddock Mousse in a Spinach Coat (for 6–8)

This is a beautiful dish. It will enhance any summer meal as part of a cold lunch or make an exciting first course for a dinner party. Young and old alike love the mild creamy filling combined with the tang of tender spinach.

1¼–1½ lb (550–675 g) large-leaved spinach
1–1¼ lb (450–550 g) finnan haddock
1 oz (25 g) unsalted butter
4 teaspoons gelatine
2 tablespoons hot water
2 eggs
lemon juice
4 tablespoons single cream

salt
cayenne pepper
thinly sliced cucumber to garnish

For the dressing
lemon juice
oil
salt, black pepper

Wash the spinach and pull the stalks off. Plunge the leaves into a saucepan with a very little boiling salted water, and stir around for only a moment or two just to make the leaves limp. Drain well, pressing with a wooden spoon to squeeze out the water. Leave on one side to cool.

Heat the oven to Gas 6/400°F/200°C. Put the fish into an ovenproof dish and dot with the butter. Cover with foil and cook in the oven for about 30 minutes until the fish is cooked. Put the gelatine and the hot water in a cup in a pan of gently simmering water and stir until the gelatine is dissolved. Remove all the flesh of the fish and discard the bones. Then put the fish and all the juices into a food processor or liquidizer with the dissolved gelatine and the yolks of the eggs. Liquidize for about ½ minute. Add a good squeeze of lemon juice and the single cream and liquidize again. Add salt and cayenne pepper to taste.

Now generously oil either 12 patty tins or a ring mould tin or flan dish. Line well with the spinach leaves, bringing them up over the edges. Now whisk the egg whites to soft peaks and fold the haddock mixture gently into them with a metal spoon. Pour the mixture into the patty tins, filling them up as high as you can. Bring the overlapping spinach leaves up over the filling and lay more on top to cover completely. Put in the fridge and chill until set.

Giving a good shake (if they are stubborn then dip the tin briefly in hot water and try again), turn out either on to individual plates or one plate and arrange very thinly sliced cucumber around them in a neatly overlapping pattern. Just before serving, make up a little simple dressing with one-third lemon juice and two-thirds oil with salt and black pepper, and spoon it over the spinach moulds.

Smoked Fish Mousse with Prawn Sauce

(for 4–5)

This pretty primrose-yellow mousse is easy to make and has the most delicate flavour and consistency combined with a rich and delicious sauce. It is served hot, either as a sustaining first course or as a light main course, accompanied by new potatoes and a green vegetable such as broad beans or broccoli.

For the mousse
peeled prawns to decorate
1 lb (450 g) smoked fish fillets, skinned
3 large egg whites
½ pint (300 ml) double or single cream
3–4 pinches cayenne pepper
salt

For the sauce
1 oz (25 g) plus 3 oz (75 g) butter
scant level tablespoon flour
½ pint (300 ml) milk
3 large egg yolks, lightly whisked
4 oz (100 g) peeled prawns
1 teaspoon tomato purée
chopped dill or fennel leaves
2–3 teaspoons white wine vinegar
cayenne pepper
salt

Generously smear a 1½–2 pint (900 ml–1·1 litre) ring mould or cake tin with butter. Arrange some prawns in a circle on the bottom of the tin. Either mince the fish fillets and then pound in a mortar until soft and pasty, or whizz in a food processor. Add the unbeaten egg whites and mix in thoroughly. Then mix in the cream. Season with cayenne pepper and salt. Put a roasting pan full of hot water on the centre shelf of the oven and heat to Gas 4/350°F/180°C. Spoon the fish mixture into the ring mould and spread evenly. Place the mould in the pan of water and cook for 20–25 minutes until firm. (If you have not made the sauce while the mousse was cooking you can switch off the oven and the mousse will stay warm sitting in the pan of water.)

To make the sauce melt 1 oz (25 g) butter in a saucepan. Remove from the heat and stir in the flour. Gradually stir in the milk. Return to the heat and bring to the boil, stirring, and let bubble, still stirring, for 2–3 minutes, until thickened and smooth. Stir in another 3 oz (75 g) butter a bit at a time. Then add the egg yolks, prawns, tomato purée, a good sprinkling of chopped dill and the wine vinegar. Season to taste with salt and cayenne pepper. To serve the dish, loosen the edges of the mousse carefully, with a knife if necessary, and turn out on to a serving plate. Pour the sauce into a sauce boat to accompany the mousse.

Fish Mousselines in Green Pea Sauce (for 4)

Here is a delicate and dreamy dish. A mixture of smoked fish, grated cheese and egg whites is dropped spoon by spoon into boiling water, and results in lightly puffed irregular balls which are served enveloped in a rich green pea sauce. Serve either as a hot first course or as a main course accompanied by new potatoes and a tomato salad.

For the mousselines
8 oz (225 g) smoked, skinned fish fillets, minced or chopped finely in a food processor
4 oz (100 g) finely grated cheese
3 large egg whites
3 tablespoons cream
¼ whole nutmeg, grated
2–3 good pinches cayenne pepper
salt

For the sauce
8 oz (225 g) green peas, fresh or frozen
3 large egg yolks
½ pint (300 ml) milk
salt, black pepper
chopped parsley, dill or fennel leaves to garnish

Put the minced fish into a bowl and pound vigorously with a large wooden spoon until pasty. Mash in the grated cheese. Thoroughly mix in the egg whites, one at a time. Stir in the cream. Season with the nutmeg, cayenne pepper and salt. Bring a large saucepan of water to a rapid boil. Take teaspoons of the fish mixture and push off the spoon into the water with your fingers. When all is used up continue boiling for 3–4 minutes. Then carefully drain the mousselines into a colander. Put them into a warm serving dish, cover loosely with foil and keep warm in a low oven while you make the sauce.

Cook the peas, drain in a sieve and rinse with cold water to cool a bit. Put them into a liquidizer with the egg yolks and milk. Whizz until smooth and then pour into a saucepan and heat gently, stirring all the time and not allowing to boil, until thickened. (This usually takes about 5 minutes. If by mistake the sauce should boil and thus curdle let it cool slightly, then put it back into the liquidizer and whizz for a moment until amalgamated once more.) Pour the sauce over the mousselines, sprinkle with chopped parsley and serve.

Mariner's Tart (for 6–8)

This is a delectable tart which can be served either as a first course or as part of a cold lunch. It is creamy rich with smoked fish, avocado and prawns, spiced subtly with mace.

For the pastry
8 oz (225 g) plain flour
good pinch salt
4 oz (100 g) butter or margarine
2 oz (50 g) lard
1 medium egg, beaten
1 tablespoon cold water

For the filling
10 oz (275 g) smoked cod

2 tablespoons olive or sunflower oil
2 oz (50 g) peeled prawns
1 avocado
1 teaspoon ground mace
1 clove garlic, crushed
½ pint (300 ml) double cream
1 medium egg, lightly beaten
juice of ½ lemon
salt, black pepper

To make the pastry, sift the flour and salt into a bowl. Cut the butter and lard into the flour and rub in lightly with your fingertips until the mixture is crumb-like. Mix in the beaten egg and the cold water with a knife. Gather up into a ball and roll out. Butter a 10–11 inch (25–28 cm) shallow flan dish (preferably the aluminium kind with a push-out base), and line the dish with the pastry, pressing a rolling pin round the edges to cut off neatly. Refrigerate the pastry-lined dish for at least 30 minutes. Heat the oven to Gas 6/400°F/200°C. To bake the tart blind, put a piece of foil across the pastry and weigh it down all over with dried beans or rice. Bake in the centre of the oven for 20–25 minutes. When cooked leave the tart to cool.

To prepare the filling, cut the fish into 1 inch (2·5 cm) pieces. Heat the oil in a frying pan and stir the fish over a gentle heat for 5–8 minutes. Transfer to a mixing bowl and add all but 2–3 of the prawns. Cut the avocado in half, peel and cut into thin slices across, and add to the mixture. Stir in the mace and garlic. Whip the cream until beginning to thicken, add the egg, lemon juice and seasoning, and continue whipping until thick. Then stir in the cool fish mixture. Heat the oven to Gas 5/375°F/190°C. Pour the creamy mixture into the pastry case and put into the centre of the oven for 15–20 minutes. Leave to cool, then decorate with the remaining prawns. This tart should be served cold but not refrigerated.

Mackerel Fillets with Parsley and Garlic (for 4–6)

In this dish the fish marinates for 24 hours but it is an extremely easy, healthy and appetizing first course. It also looks pretty as part of a cold salad lunch and is useful for a party as you can make it days ahead. Even fussy people and children hardly ever realize that the marinated fish is not cooked, and they eat it up with enthusiasm.

approx. 1¼ lb (550 g) fresh mackerel
approx. ½ pint (300 ml) white wine vinegar
2–3 large cloves garlic

good bunch parsley
3 fl oz (80 ml) sunflower oil
4 fl oz (110 ml) olive oil
salt, black pepper

Ask the fishmonger to fillet the mackerel (or do it yourself). Using a sharp knife cut the mackerel fillets into thin strips and lay them in a shallow dish. Pour over the wine vinegar, adding a little if necessary to cover the fish. Put the dish in the fridge for 2 hours. Peel and chop the garlic finely together with the parsley. Mix up in a bowl with the two oils and season well with salt and black pepper. Then drain the fish, rinse under cold water and pat dry. Lay the fish in a shallow earthenware china serving dish. Spoon the oil, parsley and garlic mixture over the fish, seeing that the strips are all well smeared with it. Cover the dish with cling film or foil and leave in the fridge for 24 hours. Serve with good brown bread, which is delicious to soak up the juices.

Marinated Fish with Avocados in Garlic and Pimento Sauce (for 6)

This delicious, healthy and unusual dish can be used either as a first course or as a light main dish for a cold lunch or supper. Don't be put off by the quantity of garlic in the sauce – when it is cooked and amalgamated with the peppers it does not taste or smell strongly at all.

1¼–1½ lb (550–675 g) skinned cod
  fillets (or other white fish)
juice of 3 lemons
wine vinegar
salt
2 large green or red peppers
olive or sunflower oil

4–5 large cloves unpeeled garlic
1 teaspoon caster sugar
cayenne pepper
2 avocados
a few lettuce leaves
chopped chives, parsley, fresh dill or
  fennel

Well beforehand, cut the fish into 1 inch (2·5 cm) chunks and lay in a large shallow but non-metallic dish. Squeeze the juice of 2 of the lemons into a measuring jug and bring it up to a little more than ¼ pint (150 ml) with wine vinegar. Stir in a teaspoon of salt and pour over the fish (if it does not cover the fish add more vinegar). Cover the dish with foil or plastic film and leave in the fridge to 'cook' for at least 3 hours (overnight is all right if convenient) until the fish is opaquely white all through.

Meanwhile cut up the peppers and fry very gently in 3 tablespoons of oil until soft. While the peppers are cooking boil the garlic cloves in water in a small saucepan. Remove the peppers from the heat and add the juice of the third lemon. Pour the mixture into a liquidizer or food processor and add the soft cloves of garlic, which will pop easily out of their skins. Whizz up and add 4–6 tablespoons oil until the sauce is smooth and fairly thick. Transfer to a bowl and season with 1 teaspoon caster sugar, salt and cayenne pepper to taste. Leave to cool and then refrigerate.

When the fish is white, strain off the juices and rinse the fish under cold water. Stir the fish pieces into the cold sauce. Cut the avocados in half, scoop out in teaspoonfuls and add to the fish and sauce. To serve, spoon the mixture on to lettuce leaves on individual plates or one large plate, and sprinkle with a little cayenne pepper and chopped chives, parsley, dill or fennel.

Ceviche (for 6–8)

Few courses can be so easy, original and appetizing as this dish from South America. I first tasted ceviche when I lived in Peru as a child, and never realized that the tender aromatic pieces of white fish were in fact raw. It is marinated in a combination of fresh lemon and lime juice, and the acid in the juices actually 'cooks' the fish as it sits in the fridge. I find that fresh chopped root ginger as an alternative to the traditional ground chilli gives an irresistible flavour. If you can't get fresh limes use just lemon juice.

1½–1¾ lb (675–800 g) skinned, filleted white fish (I use haddock or cod)
1 inch (2·5 cm) piece fresh ginger or ½ teaspoon ground chilli
2 cloves garlic
1 teaspoon salt

black pepper
½–¾ pint (300–450 ml) mixed fresh lemon and lime juice
crisp lettuce
1 onion (preferably the deep red kind)
fresh dill (optional)

Cut the fish into 1 inch (2·5 cm) pieces and arrange on the bottom of a glass or ceramic dish. Peel the ginger and the garlic, chop up finely, and mix in a bowl with the salt, a few grindings of black pepper and the lemon and lime juice. Pour the mixture over the fish – if the liquid does not cover it add some more lemon juice. Cover the dish with foil or cling film, and refrigerate for at least 3 hours until the fish is quite white and looks cooked.

Before serving arrange a bed of crisp lettuce leaves on a pretty, shallow plate. Take the pieces of fish from the marinade and arrange them on the lettuce leaves. Slice the onion as finely as possible in rings and scatter over the fish. During the summer I sprinkle chopped fresh dill over as well, as it has such a wonderful affinity with cold fish. A variation of this dish is to put some sliced avocado among the fish and spoon over a little French dressing.

Marinated Fish Salad with Fresh Ginger (for 4)

An aromatic main course salad or an unusual first course. It is best to make it several hours ahead, or even the day before, so that the lovely flavour of the spices really penetrates the fish and prawns. The fish is 'cooked' by the acids in the lemon juice.

1 lb (450 g) cod fillets, skinned
2 inch (5 cm) piece fresh ginger
2–3 cloves garlic
1 tablespoon tomato purée
¼ pint (150 ml) lemon juice
½ teaspoon ground cardamom or coriander
pinch ground chilli

salt
4–6 oz (100–175 g) prawns

For the garnish
chicory or other attractive leaves
natural yogurt
½ bunch spring onions, finely chopped

Cut the fish into 2 inch (5 cm) chunks. Peel and finely chop the ginger and garlic. Put the tomato purée and lemon juice into a saucepan and heat until bubbling, then stir in the chopped ginger and garlic together with the ground cardamom and chilli and a sprinkling of salt. Cover the pan and bubble gently for 5 minutes. Then add the sliced fish and the prawns to the pan and stir gently but thoroughly into the mixture. Remove from the heat, cover the pan again, and leave at room temperature for a few hours, or overnight in the fridge.

Empty the contents of the pan carefully into a colander to drain off the excess juices. Arrange the chicory leaves prettily either on individual plates or on one serving dish. Pile the fish mixture in the centre and top with a little yogurt. Scatter the spring onions all over and serve very cold.

Monkfish Salad with Exotic Sauce (for 10)

This can be either a first course or one of the dishes at a cold meal. People seem to like it so much that they almost lick the last remaining juices off their plates – serve plenty of good bread so that they don't have to resort to this! Monkfish has a firm, meaty texture and is said to be like scampi. I think it is often better. If you cannot get fresh coriander leaves (which by the way are well worth growing from seed), use continental parsley or mint leaves.

2½ lb (1·25 kg) monkfish	2 teaspoons caster sugar
4 tablespoons olive oil	1 tablespoon tomato purée
2 large green chillies	juice of ½ lemon
2–3 cloves garlic	salt
1 lb (450 g) tomatoes	good bunch fresh coriander leaves
1 rounded teaspoon ground cardamom	4 oz (100 g) firm mushrooms
	1 small cos lettuce

Cut the monkfish into approximately 1½ inch (3·5 cm) chunks, cutting out any bones. Heat the oil in a large frying pan and cook the fish over a medium heat for 5–7 minutes, turning round gently. Turn off the heat, remove the pieces of fish with a slotted spoon, and leave them on one side in a mixing bowl. Leave the fish juices in the frying pan.

Cut the chillies open under running water and discard the seeds. Chop up the chillies and garlic finely. Pour boiling water over the tomatoes, leave for a minute or two, and then peel them and chop up finely. Now pour any juices that have drained from the fish in the mixing bowl back into the frying pan. Bring the juices to the boil and add the chilli, garlic, cardamom, chopped tomatoes, sugar, tomato purée and lemon juice. Stir around and bubble gently over a low heat for 7–10 minutes until the tomatoes are soft. Season to taste with salt and turn off the heat. Chop up about three-quarters of the coriander leaves and stir them into the hot sauce. Then pour the sauce over the fish in the bowl and gently mix in. Lastly, slice the mushrooms across fairly thinly and stir them into the mixture. Leave until cold.

When completely cold arrange cos lettuce leaves on a serving dish and spoon the fish mixture into the centre. Pull the whole leaves off the remaining sprigs of coriander and scatter them over the dish. Serve as soon as possible, meanwhile keep in a very cool place but not the fridge.

Monkfish with Avocados in Dill Mayonnaise (for 6)

This makes an appetizing first course. Alternatively, accompanied by crisp salad and perhaps some cold new potatoes tossed in a vinaigrette dressing, it is a lovely cold lunch or supper.

1¾ lb (800 g) filleted monkfish
2 egg yolks
½ pint (300 ml) olive or sunflower oil
1 tablespoon wine vinegar
1 carton soured cream
2 cloves garlic, crushed

1 tablespoon fresh or dried dill, finely chopped
salt, black pepper
2 large avocados
a little cayenne

Cut the fish into largish chunks. Put the pieces into a steamer over simmering water and cover. The fish should be white and cooked within about 10 minutes. Allow to cool.

Whisk the egg yolks together with 1 tablespoon of the oil, and then add the rest of the oil drop by drop at first, then in a very thin stream, whisking (or whizzing in a liquidizer) all the time until you have a rather stiff mayonnaise. Whisk in the wine vinegar and add the soured cream, crushed garlic, chopped dill, and salt and black pepper to taste. Scoop out the avocados and mix into the mayonnaise gently, together with the fish. Spoon into a pretty serving dish and sprinkle with a little cayenne pepper. If keeping in the fridge before eating, cover the dish lightly with plastic film.

Main Courses

Pancakes Stuffed with Leeks, Onions and Almonds (for 6–8)

This is a scrumptious dish which is equally popular with both adults and children and very useful if you have vegetarians in the house. It takes a little time to make as it must be done in stages, but can then be kept hot in a low oven for several hours and needs only a crisp green vegetable such as broccoli to accompany it.

For the batter
4 oz (100 g) plain flour
2 eggs
½ teaspoon salt
2 oz (50 g) butter
½ pint (300 ml) milk

For the filling
2 lb (900 g) leeks
2 large onions
butter
2–3 oz (50–75 g) whole blanched
  almonds
salt, black pepper

For the sauce
1 pint (600 ml) white sauce
3 oz (75 g) grated cheese
1 large egg, well beaten
1–2 tablespoons very hot water
¼ nutmeg, freshly ground
salt, black pepper
grated Parmesan cheese
a little butter

Make a rich pancake batter by putting the flour, eggs and salt in a food processor or liquidizer. Melt the butter, pour it into the cold milk and add the mixture to the flour and egg. Whizz up together for about 1 minute until smooth, scraping down any flour which may stick to the sides. Leave the batter to sit in a cool place while you make the filling.

Now wash and prepare the leeks and slice in rounds. Peel the onions and slice up into fairly small pieces. Melt a generous piece of butter in a large pan. Put in the onions and leeks and stir about over a gentle heat until soft. Meanwhile, fry the almonds in a little butter and add to the leek and onion mixture. Season with salt and black pepper to taste. Remove from the heat and cover the pan.

Now cook the pancakes, laying them on top of each other on a plate as you do them. Then take a large, rather shallow, ovenproof dish and lay the pancakes in it one by one, spooning some of the leek filling into each and rolling them round. Cover the dish with foil and put in a very low oven to keep warm.

Make the white sauce and stir in the grated cheese. When the cheese is melted, take off the heat and whisk in the beaten egg. Then whisk in the hot water to lighten the sauce. Add the ground nutmeg and salt and black pepper to taste. Pour the sauce over the pancakes, sprinkle generously with grated Parmesan, dot with butter and put under a hot grill until browned. Then keep hot in a low oven until you are ready to eat.

Golden Orient Eggs (for 3–4)

These make a delicious supper or lunch dish accompanied by rice and a firm green vegetable such as broccoli. The hard-boiled eggs are covered in a golden yellow sauce made with rich coconut milk flavoured with onion and tomato and spiced with turmeric and chilli.

4 oz (100 g) unsweetened desiccated coconut
1 pint (600 ml) milk
6 eggs
1 medium onion
1 clove garlic
1 large squashy tomato

1 oz (25 g) butter or margarine
1 teaspoon ground turmeric
½–1 teaspoon chilli powder
salt
finely chopped spring onions to garnish

Put the coconut into a bowl. Bring the milk to the boil, pour on to the coconut, stir, and leave for about 20 minutes. Meanwhile medium hard-boil the eggs. Shell them and cut in half. Peel and finely chop the onion and garlic. Pour boiling water over the tomato, peel it and chop finely.

Melt the butter in a frying pan, add the onion and garlic and cook gently, stirring around until soft and golden, then add the tomato and cook until softened. Strain the milk from the coconut into a jug through a fine sieve, pressing to extract all the liquid. Gradually stir the milk into the frying pan mixture. Add the turmeric, the chilli and salt to taste. Bring to the boil and bubble for a minute. Pour the mixture into a liquidizer or food processor and whizz until smooth. Return the sauce to the pan and add the halved eggs. Bubble gently for 2–3 minutes and then put into a warmed serving dish. Just before serving, sprinkle with the spring onions.

Billowed Eggs (for 4)

This pretty dish tastes like a cheese soufflé but is quicker to make and sure not to fail. It is a simple but rich dish and I like it best with a slightly bitter chicory or curly endive salad.

For the cheese sauce
1 oz (25 g) butter or margarine
½ oz (15 g) plain flour, sifted
½ pint (300 ml) milk
2–3 oz (50–75 g) grated cheese

2–3 teaspoons Dijon mustard
salt
cayenne pepper

4 large eggs
pinch salt

First make the cheese sauce. Melt the butter in a saucepan, remove from the heat and thoroughly stir in the sifted flour. Gradually stir in the milk, return to the heat and bring to the boil, stirring all the time. Then simmer, still stirring, for about 3 minutes. Add the grated cheese and the mustard and stir until the cheese has melted. Lastly, add the salt and a little cayenne pepper to taste. Cover the pan and keep the sauce warm.

Butter an ovenproof dish. Heat the oven to Gas 7/425°F/220°C. Separate the yolks from the whites of the eggs, carefully keeping the yolks whole. Whisk the egg whites until getting thick, add a good pinch of salt and continue whisking until the whites stand in peaks. Spoon into the ovenproof dish. Make four holes in the egg white and drop in the egg yolks. Bake just above the centre of the oven for 7–10 minutes until the yolks are just softly set. Serve at once and pour the cheese sauce over the top at the table.

Spiced Spinach with Eggs and Fresh Ginger (for 4)

A most delicious dish which you can rustle up for a more exciting lunch or supper. We eat it with warm wholemeal bread or with flat pitta breads.

1¾–2 lb (800–900 g) spinach, fresh or frozen

1 inch (2·5 cm) piece fresh ginger, peeled

1 small green chilli, cut open and seeded, *or* ¼–½ teaspoon chilli powder

3 large cloves garlic, peeled
sunflower oil

2 oz (50 g) butter or margarine

2 heaped teaspoons ground coriander

1 heaped teaspoon ground cumin

½ teaspoon ground cloves

3 tablespoons lemon juice
salt

4 large eggs

1 teaspoon paprika

Wash the spinach and remove the stems. Chop the ginger, the seeded chilli and the garlic together finely. Cook the spinach in a little salted water for just a minute or two until limp (if using frozen spinach, just thaw and drain). Drain well and press out excess water. Cut the spinach up finely. Put a fairly large, shallow serving dish in a low oven to get warm.

Heat 1 tablespoon oil and 1 oz (25 g) of the butter in a large frying pan. Stir in the chopped ginger and chilli, the garlic and the spices and stir around over the heat for a minute or two. Then add the spinach and the lemon juice and stir around over a gentle heat for 5–8 minutes. Season to taste with salt and spread the spinach out in the warm serving dish.

Put a tablespoon more oil in the pan and fry the eggs, 2 at a time, basting with the oil until the white is only just set. Arrange the eggs on the bed of spinach. Finally melt the remaining 1 oz (25 g) butter in a small saucepan, stir in the paprika, and trickle this red liquid over the eggs just before serving.

Stuffed Peppers Gratinée (for 4–6)

All my family love this delicious variation of a well-known dish. The pepper 'boats' are stuffed with a rich beef, tomato and sage mixture, and then topped with a golden cheese sauce flavoured with Parmesan. They cook in the oven on a bed of tomato and onion and are good served with sauté potatoes and French beans.

just over 1 oz (25 g) butter or margarine

1 heaped tablespoon plain flour

¼ pint (150 ml) milk

4 oz (100 g) grated cheese
salt, black pepper

grated Parmesan cheese	2 tablespoons tomato purée
12 oz (350 g) minced beef	1 teaspoon paprika
2 oz (50 g) fresh breadcrumbs	1 large onion
2–3 cloves garlic, finely chopped	2 large tomatoes
1 tablespoon sage leaves, finely chopped	3 medium-sized green peppers

First make the topping. Melt 1 oz (25 g) of the butter or margarine in a saucepan, then remove from the heat and stir in the flour. Gradually blend in the milk. Return to the heat and bring to the boil, stirring all the time. Let the sauce bubble, still stirring, for 2–3 minutes. It should be very thick. Then stir in the grated cheese and remove from the heat. Stir until the cheese has melted and the sauce is smooth, then season to taste with salt and black pepper. Stir in a generous sprinkling of grated Parmesan and put on one side to cool.

Mix the minced beef in a bowl with the breadcrumbs, chopped garlic, sage, tomato purée and paprika. Season very well with salt and black pepper. Peel the onion and slice very finely in rings. Pour boiling water over the tomatoes, skin them and chop them up into very small pieces. Spread the onions and tomatoes on the bottom of a fairly large ovenproof dish and season with salt and pepper.

Cut the peppers in half lengthways and remove the seeds and stalks. Bring a large pan of salted water to the boil and boil the pepper halves for 8–10 minutes, just to soften them a little. Drain, and then spoon the meat mixture into the pepper halves, patting it down to fill them tightly. Lay the peppers on top of the onion and tomato mixture. Spoon the thick cheese sauce on top of each pepper, completely covering the meat. Sprinkle with more grated Parmesan and dot generously with the remaining butter. Heat the oven to Gas 4/350°F/180°C, and cook uncovered in the centre of the oven for 1 hour.

Hot Stuffed Avocados Gratinée (for 4)

These are a real treat. There is a lot to be said for serving avocados hot, either sliced and briefly sautéed in butter to add to other vegetables, or as in this recipe where they make an unusual main course. Here they are stuffed with pork in a sweet red pepper purée and topped with cheese. They are decorative and delicious. I would serve them with new or sautéed potatoes and either broad beans, petits pois or a salad.

2 medium-sized red peppers	8 oz (225 g) minced pork
4 large unpeeled cloves of garlic	1 teaspoon oregano
1 tablespoon lemon juice	4 large avocados
salt, black pepper	3 oz (75 g) grated cheese
1 medium onion	parsley sprigs to decorate
2 tablespoons olive oil	

First cut the red peppers up roughly. Put into a pan of boiling water with the cloves of garlic, cover, and simmer for 10 minutes. Drain. Peel the garlic (it will almost pop out of its skin) and put into a liquidizer with the red peppers and the lemon juice. Season with salt and black pepper and whizz to a purée. Leave on one side.

Peel the onion and chop up. Heat the olive oil in a frying pan and fry gently until softened. Season the minced pork with salt and pepper and add to the pan with the oregano. Stir over the heat for 4–8 minutes until the pork is cooked, and then add the pepper and garlic purée and bubble for a minute or two more. Check the seasoning (it should be highly seasoned for it to combine well with the bland avocado). Heat the oven to Gas 5/375°F/190°C.

Cut the avocados in half, remove the stones, and smear the flesh with lemon juice to avoid discolouration. Put into a shallow ovenproof dish. Pile the mince mixture into the avocados, spreading it all over the top as well as into the holes. Then pile the grated cheese on top of the mince. Cook in the centre of the oven for 15–20 minutes. Before serving decorate the dish with sprigs of parsley between the avocados.

Green Noodles with Cream of Red Pepper Sauce (for 4–5)

An irresistible dish. This is a mixture of green spinach noodles, tender slivers of chicken breast and prawns, coated in a smooth and luscious red pepper and cream sauce incorporating small crunchy rings of courgettes. The contrast of the green noodles and the flame-coloured sauce is very enticing. Serve it with a tomato salad and good bread. In summer, fresh chopped leaf fennel or dill is excellent added to the sauce.

2–3 red peppers
4–5 large cloves garlic
8–10 oz (225–275 g) chicken breast
 fillets, skinned
2 oz (50 g) butter
8 oz (225 g) peeled prawns

salt, black pepper
8–10 oz (225–275 g) green noodles
 (tagliatelle)
½ pint (300 ml) single cream
8–10 oz (225–275 g) small courgettes
grated Parmesan cheese

First cut up the red peppers roughly, removing the seeds. Put into a saucepan of water with the unpeeled cloves of garlic. Cover the pan, bring to the boil, then simmer for 15–20 minutes until soft. Drain the pepper and garlic and leave on one side.

Slice the chicken breast into thin, small pieces. Heat the butter in a pan and fry the chicken pieces gently for 8–10 minutes until cooked. Stir in the prawns, season with salt and pepper and remove from the heat. Put the noodles in a pan of boiling salted water and cook for about 8 minutes. Meanwhile put the cooked pepper into a food processor or liquidizer with the cloves of garlic, squeezed out of their skins, and the cream. Whizz until smooth, and season with salt and black pepper. Transfer the sauce to a largish saucepan and heat up. Add the sliced courgettes and let bubble for no more than a minute.

When the noodles are ready, drain them and put into a large heated serving dish. Re-heat the chicken and prawns in the pan and spoon on top of the noodles, pouring in their juices. Lastly pour over the red pepper and courgette sauce and serve immediately. Pass round a bowl of grated Parmesan to sprinkle over the noodles on your plate.

Green Noodles with Mussels and Tarragon (for 4)

I adore fresh mussels, and nothing could be much more delicious than combining them with spinach-flavoured noodles and a creamy sauce. It makes fewer mussels go a long way so you have less to clean. It's also a simple meal to serve, as everyone will be completely satisfied if the noodles are just accompanied by a crisp green salad.

2 quarts (2·3 litres) fresh mussels
2 large cloves garlic, finely
 chopped
2 oz (50 g) butter
salt, black pepper

2 teaspoons finely chopped fresh
 tarragon
5 fl oz (150 ml) single cream
¾ lb (350 g) green noodles
grated Parmesan cheese

If time allows, soak the mussels for several hours in cold water sprinkled with flour or oatmeal – in this way the mussels are said to eat the flour and cleanse themselves. Discard any mussels which are already open or which float to the top. Scrub the mussels clean, but in this recipe there is no need to pull the beard off them. Then put them in a large saucepan with ½ inch (1 cm) of water in the bottom. Cover it and bring to the boil. After about a minute, or when all the mussels are open, drain them and remove them from their shells. Discard any mussels which have not opened. Put them in a dish with the chopped garlic, a generous 2 oz (50 g) butter, salt and black pepper. Cover the dish and keep warm in a very low oven together with a large dish ready for the noodles.

Stir the chopped tarragon into the cream, add salt and plenty of black pepper and keep on one side. Cook the noodles in plenty of boiling salted water for 6–10 minutes until just soft. Drain and put into the large hot dish. Stir in the tarragon cream and a generous sprinkling of Parmesan. Lastly, roughly stir in the mussels and their garlic buttery juices, leaving several mussels near the top to look appetizing. Sprinkle again with Parmesan and serve.

Gnocchi Wrapped in Bacon (for 6)

These cheesy semolina gnocchi are a perfect family dish. Firstly they are delicious, secondly they can be made well in advance and kept in the fridge, or cooked and kept warm for an hour or two in a low oven. They make an excellent lunch or supper dish and are especially good with broccoli.

4 oz (100 g) fine semolina
1 pint (600 ml) milk
3 oz (75 g) grated cheese
1 oz (25 g) butter
¼ whole nutmeg, grated
salt to taste

2–3 pinches cayenne pepper
1 egg, whisked
6 oz (175 g) smoked streaky bacon,
  finely sliced with the rind cut off
grated Parmesan cheese

Put the semolina and milk into a saucepan. Bring to the boil and allow to simmer gently, stirring all the time with a wooden spoon, for about 3 minutes until very thick. Then remove from the heat and add the grated cheese, the butter, the grated nutmeg, salt and cayenne pepper to taste. Then thoroughly stir in the whisked egg. Leave to become completely cold.

Butter a fairly large shallow ovenproof dish. Using floured hands, take up small handfuls of the semolina mixture and roll into sausages about 2½ inches (6·5 cm) long. Roll a piece of bacon roughly round each one, leaving gaps of semolina still exposed. Lay the gnocchi closely together in the dish and sprinkle all over with grated Parmesan. Heat the oven to Gas 8/450°F/230°C and put the dish towards the top of the oven for 20–30 minutes until golden brown.

Spaghetti with Walnut and Parsley Sauce (for 4)

This nutty sauce for spaghetti or noodles has an unusual and delicious flavour. Both adults and children seem to like it, accompanied by a simple green salad.

2 oz (50 g) walnuts
1 large clove garlic
handful fresh parsley
5 tablespoons olive or sunflower oil

2 tablespoons very hot water
salt, black pepper
8 oz (225 g) spaghetti

Grind the walnuts roughly in a food processor or with a pestle and mortar. Chop the garlic and the parsley finely together. Gently heat 2 tablespoons of the oil in a pan, add the garlic and parsley and turn around for a moment over a low heat. Add the ground nuts and cook a little but don't brown. Then stir in 3 more tablespoons of oil and 2 tablespoons of very hot water. Season well with salt and black pepper. Leave in the pan while you boil the spaghetti in salted water until done. Then drain, and mix the sauce thoroughly into the spaghetti.

Quick Pizza (for 4)

A true pizza is made with yeast dough, but it takes time, and I find that if I use soda bread dough I can put a steaming home-made pizza on the table in a little over half an hour, which is perfect for an easy lunch or children's supper. You can alter the topping to your taste or according to what bits and pieces you have around.

8 oz (225 g) strong white bread flour
1 level teaspoon bicarbonate of soda
1 level teaspoon cream of tartar
1 level teaspoon salt
¼ pint (150 ml) milk, soured with 1
  tablespoon vinegar
olive or sunflower oil

2 tablespoons tomato purée
3–4 oz (75–100 g) ham, chopped
2 oz (50 g) mushrooms, finely sliced
1 heaped teaspoon oregano
1 large tomato, sliced in small pieces
2–3 oz (50–75 g) grated cheese
black pepper

Sift the flour, bicarbonate of soda, cream of tartar and salt into a bowl. Stir in the soured milk and mix with a wooden spoon or electric dough hook to a soft but manageable dough, adding a little more milk if necessary. Turn on to a floured surface, knead lightly, and form the dough into a ball. Roll into a circle 11–12 inches (27·5–30 cm) in diameter.

Heat the oven to Gas 6/400°F/200°C. Put the dough on to a greased baking sheet or large tin plate, and brush all over with oil. Mix the tomato purée with a tablespoon of oil and spread on the dough to within about 1 inch (2·5 cm) of the edge. Sprinkle with the ham, mushrooms, oregano and tomato. Top with grated cheese, sprinkle with black pepper, and spoon over another tablespoon of oil. Bake in the centre of the oven for 20–25 minutes until the base is risen at the edges and browned.

Fried Pizza (for 4–6)

For children's suppers or weekend lunches this home-made pizza is always popular. You can vary the topping according to what you have or like, this recipe being just an example. We specially like all kinds of cooked or smoked fish. A topping of seafood and prawns, with tomatoes, fresh chopped fennel leaves and slices of Mozarella cheese, is delicious. Just be inventive.

6 oz (175 g) strong plain flour
1 heaped teaspoon salt
3 teaspoons baking powder
6–7 tablespoons cold water
4 oz (100 g) Bel Paese or Cheddar
  cheese, cut into cubes
2 oz (50 g) ham, cut into small pieces

1 small onion, cut very finely in rings
2 small to medium tomatoes
3–4 tablespoons olive oil
1 teaspoon oregano
1 oz (25 g) butter
salt, black pepper

Sift the flour, salt and baking powder into a mixing bowl. Stir in the cold water and mix to a stiff dough. Knead lightly on a floured board for a few minutes. Prepare the cheese, ham and onions. Pour boiling water over the tomatoes, then peel and cut across into thin slices. Keep the topping ingredients on one side. Knead the dough for a moment more and then roll out into a circle 8–9 inches (20–23 cm) in diameter.

Heat the olive oil in a large frying pan until beginning to sizzle. Put in the circle of dough and turn the heat down to moderate. Cook for 4–5 minutes until the pizza is golden on the under side. Turn over, turn the heat to very low, and pile on the topping ingredients, finishing with the cheese and oregano and dotting with butter. Sprinkle with salt and black pepper. Cover the pan as tightly as you can with a piece of foil and continue cooking for 10–12 minutes until the topping ingredients have softened and the cheese is melted. Transfer the pizza with a spatula to a serving plate, and if not yet ready to eat, keep warm in a low oven.

Ravishing Roulade (for 5–6)

This is a kind of savoury Swiss roll. Both fun and easy to make, it is a divine combination of pork fillet, turkey breast and ham, interspersed with a mixture of parsley, garlic, green peppercorns and anchovies. During the summer it is delightful eaten cold, sliced very thinly.

12 oz (350 g) pork fillet
10–12 oz (275–350 g) turkey or
  chicken breast fillets, skinned
large handful parsley
1–2 cloves garlic
1 rounded teaspoon green
  peppercorns

1 tin anchovies
4 oz (100 g) sliced ham
lemon juice
olive oil
¼ pint (150 ml) single cream
salt, black pepper

Lay the pork fillet on a sheet of greaseproof paper – slice into the meat lengthways to open it out, but don't cut right through it. Lay another piece of greaseproof paper on top and bang the meat out forcefully with a rolling pin, as thinly as possible. Then, in the same way, bang out the turkey fillets. Finely chop the parsley, garlic, green peppercorns and anchovies and mix together, including the anchovy oil. Lay out the bashed-out pork fillet and spread with one-third of the parsley mixture. Then put the turkey breasts on top, spread on more parsley mixture, and lastly lay on the slices of ham and smear with the remaining parsley mixture. Now roll up, starting from the short side like a Swiss roll. Carefully place the roll, join side down, in a roasting pan and smear all over with lemon juice and olive oil.

Heat the oven to Gas 2/300°F/150°C. Lay a piece of foil loosely over the meat and roast in the centre of the oven for 1¾–2 hours, basting occasionally and removing the foil about half-way through the cooking time. Move the meat carefully to a carving board, slice in fairly thin slices, and lay neatly in a warm serving dish. Bubble up the pan juices for a minute or two until reduced and thickened a bit, then stir in the cream and heat up. Finally, stir in 2–3 teaspoons of lemon juice and season to taste with salt and black pepper. Serve in a warm sauceboat to pour over the meat.

Sautéed Kidneys with Mushrooms (for 2)

This is a good dish which I often make at the end of a busy day for our supper because it is so quick. If you are lucky enough to find a calf's kidney instead of the lambs' kidneys, snap it up because it will be specially delicious.

4 lambs' kidneys	2 teaspoons oregano
butter or margarine	2 teaspoons mild French mustard
1 onion, finely sliced	4 oz (100 g) mushrooms, sliced
1 tablespoon tomato ketchup	salt, black pepper
½ wineglass sherry	chopped parsley

Slice the kidneys thinly and fry gently in a little butter for about 5 minutes only. Transfer them to a serving dish and keep warm. Cook the sliced onion in the remaining pan juices until soft, adding a little more butter if necessary. Stir in the tomato ketchup, sherry, oregano and mustard. Then add the sliced mushrooms and bubble for just a minute or two until the mushrooms are just cooked. Season to taste. Pour the pan mixture over the kidneys, sprinkle with a little parsley, and serve. If you want to have potatoes as well as a green vegetable, mashed are good for the sauce to seep into.

Sweetbreads in Piquant Butter Sauce

(for 4)

A mild and tender dish in which the sweetbreads and butter magically combine to make their own rich and creamy sauce with the subtle zest of fresh chilli. Serve with plain rice and a crisp green vegetable so as not to detract from the delicate flavour.

1 lb (450 g) calves' or lambs' sweetbreads	2 large onions
1 tablespoon vinegar	3 oz (75 g) butter
1 small green chilli	salt
1 small red chilli	parsley to garnish

Soak the sweetbreads in water for an hour or two, changing the water once or twice to get rid of all traces of blood. For the final 30 minutes of soaking, add the vinegar to the water. Cut the chillies open under running water, discarding the stalks and seeds, and chop up finely. Peel the onions and slice in rings.

Melt 2 oz (50 g) of the butter in a large, heavy frying pan and fry the onions over medium heat. When the onions are soft and golden, add the chopped chillies and fry, stirring around, for about a minute. Add the remaining 1 oz (25 g) of butter and turn the heat as low as possible. Drain the sweetbreads and add them to the pan. Put a piece of foil or a lid over the pan and cook, stirring around occasionally, for 10–15 minutes. Season to taste with salt and transfer to a warm serving dish. (If necessary cover the dish and keep warm in a very low oven until you are ready to eat.) Just before serving, sprinkle with chopped parsley.

Green Dragon Walnut Meat Balls (for 4)

These have a definitely oriental character with their glossy sweet and sour sauce. They are quick to prepare, and make an excellent lunch or supper dish served with flat egg noodles and a green salad. My young unmarried sister had a great success when she gave a large party and fed everyone with a mountain of these tasty meat balls.

For the meat balls
1 large green pepper
1 lb (450 g) minced beef or pork
2 cloves garlic, finely chopped
1–2 inch (2·5–5 cm) piece fresh
  ginger, peeled and finely chopped
3 oz (75 g) walnuts, chopped
1 tablespoon tomato purée
2 tablespoons soy sauce
3–4 pinches cayenne pepper

1 tablespoon caster sugar
salt
1 tablespoon sunflower oil for frying

For the sauce
1 tablespoon soy sauce
3 tablespoons water
2 teaspoons wine vinegar
½ tablespoon caster sugar
3–4 spring onions, finely chopped

Cut the green pepper in half and take out the seeds and stem. Bring a small pan of salted water to the boil, put in the pepper, cover the pan and boil for 6–8 minutes until soft. Drain and chop finely. Put the minced meat into a bowl, and add the chopped pepper, chopped garlic and ginger, walnuts, tomato purée and soy sauce. Then add the cayenne pepper, caster sugar and a good sprinkling of salt. Mix all well together with a wooden spoon. Then, using wet hands, form into ping-pong sized balls. Heat the sunflower oil in a large frying pan and fry the balls over a low to medium heat, turning around all over, for about 20 minutes. Transfer with a slotted spoon to a serving dish and keep warm in a low oven.

Pour most of the fat out of the pan but leave the residue of meat juices. Add the soy sauce, water and vinegar. Stir in the caster sugar and dissolve over a low heat. Then bubble fiercely for a minute or two until you have a thick, dark and syrupy sauce. Remove from the heat and stir in the chopped spring onions. Spoon the sauce over the meat balls and serve at once.

Indian Spiced Meat Balls Stuffed with Curd Cheese (for 4–5)

These aromatic meat balls have a soft filling of curd cheese. They make a good summer meal arranged on a bed of fresh mint leaves and served with a salad and bread.

1 lb (450 g) finely minced beef
2 teaspoons coriander seeds
8 cardamom pods
6–8 whole cloves

3–4 pinches chilli powder
3–4 cloves garlic, finely chopped
1 egg, beaten
4 oz (100 g) curd cheese

1 tablespoon oil	**chopped mint leaves or parsley to**
salt	**garnish**

Put the minced beef into a bowl and mash with a large wooden spoon until pasty. Grind the coriander seeds, the cardamom seeds (discarding the pods) and the cloves in a coffee grinder or a pestle and mortar. When the spices are ground add them to the beef with the chilli powder and garlic and season with salt. Thoroughly mix in the beaten egg. With wet hands, form the mixture into small balls, the size of a ping-pong ball, and then flatten out into circles on an oiled surface. Put a teaspoon of curd cheese on each circle and carefully bring the meat up and around to encase the cheese completely, thus making the meat balls larger than before.

Heat the oil in a large frying pan and fry the meat balls over a medium heat for about 5–7 minutes on each side, until brown. Transfer to a serving dish and sprinkle with mint or parsley.

Curried Beef Surprise Cake (for 4)

There is something magical about this dish. The surprise is the running softness of the poached eggs as you cut into the centre of the juicy cake. The magic is that the poached eggs retain their softness and don't continue cooking with the beef. It makes a good lunch or supper dish, served with either rice or mashed potatoes and a green vegetable or simply with salad and good bread.

4 medium eggs	**handful fresh mint leaves, finely**
1 lb (450 g) minced beef	**chopped**
2–3 teaspoons curry powder	**salt**
2–3 cloves garlic, finely chopped	**oil**
1 tablespoon Worcestershire sauce	

Poach the eggs lightly in a poacher until the whites are just set, then plunge them into cold water to cool them and prevent further cooking. Put the beef in a bowl and mix in the curry powder, garlic, Worcestershire sauce and mint. Season with salt. Spread half the mixture in a 6 inch (15 cm) diameter cake tin (not one with a loose base), pressing it down with a wooden spoon. Then make four depressions in the mince and put in the poached eggs. Cover with the remaining mince, again pressing it down lightly with a spoon. Brush the top with oil.

Heat the oven to Gas 9/475°F/240°C and be sure that it has reached its maximum heat before putting in the cake. Cook the cake towards the top of the oven for 15–20 minutes. Pour the juices out of the tin into a small saucepan, and boil fiercely over a high heat for 2–4 minutes until reduced to a syrupy glaze. Turn the cake out carefully and place on a serving dish, top side up. Spoon the reduced juices over the cake and serve.

Leek and Beef Patties with Lemon Sauce (for 6)

These are very moist and soft meat balls, infused with a sharp lemon sauce which mingles well with the subtle flavour of the leeks. These patties go well with a dish of buttered noodles or spaghetti. The recipe is also delicious using spinach (1½–2 lb (675 g–1 kg)) instead of the leeks.

1½lb (675 g) leeks	2 oz (50 g) butter
12 oz (350 g) minced beef	juice of 2 lemons
2 oz (50 g) ground rice	½ pint (300 ml) water
2 eggs, beaten	1 tablespoon finely chopped mint or
salt, black pepper	parsley
1 tablespoon sunflower oil	

Removing any tough outer leaves, wash the leeks carefully. Cut them into two or three pieces each, put in a pan of boiling, salted water, and boil for 4–5 minutes, until just tender. Drain and then chop very finely. Pound the meat in a bowl with a large wooden spoon until pasty (or simply whizz for a moment or two in a food processor). Add the ground rice, chopped leeks and beaten eggs. Season well with salt and black pepper and mix thoroughly with a wooden spoon. Lightly form the rather soft mixture into small balls, roughly the size of ping-pong balls.

Heat the sunflower oil and 1 oz (25 g) of the butter in a large frying pan. Fry the patties over a fairly high heat, turning gently with a small spatula just to brown, then put the pan on one side. Put the lemon juice, the remaining butter and the water in a large saucepan and season well with salt and black pepper. Bring to the boil, add the patties, cover, and simmer for 20 minutes, stirring gently now and then. Remove the patties with a slotted spoon to a heated serving dish. Bubble the remaining juices up fiercely for a moment or two until reduced and thickened. Stir in the chopped mint or parsley and pour the sauce over the patties just before serving.

Rolled Beef with Cheese and Sage (for 6–8)

A delicious way of cooking stewing beef, easy, quick and quite fun to make. Ask the butcher to cut the beef into slices like frying steak. The mingling of flavours with the melted cheese is very good. I usually serve layered potatoes and onions cooked in the oven with this, and a green vegetable.

2 lb (900 g) stewing beef, cut into thin
  steaks
handful sage leaves
3 large cloves garlic, peeled
6 oz (175 g) Jarlsberg or Edam cheese

tomato purée
salt, black pepper
1 large glass red wine
1 heaped tablespoon cornflour
1 carton soured cream

Lay out the pieces of beef, giving a bash with a rolling pin to any that look a bit thick. Chop the sage and garlic together very finely. Slice the cheese thinly into as many slices as there are of beef. Smear each piece of beef generously with tomato purée and sprinkle with salt and black pepper. Lay on a slice of cheese and then pat on the finely chopped sage and garlic. Roll each piece of beef over and secure with a toothpick. Lay the beef rolls in an iron casserole dish. Heat the oven to Gas 2/300°F/150°C.

Pour over the red wine and enough water to three-quarters cover the beef. Bring to the boil on top of the stove, then cover and cook in the oven for 1¾–2½ hours until the meat feels tender when you stick a knife into it. Drain the juices from the meat and put into a saucepan. Mix the cornflour with a little water until smooth and add to the juices. Bring to the boil, stirring, and bubble for 3–4 minutes. Pour the sauce back over the beef, and top with the soured cream before serving.

Beef Stuffed with Smoked Oysters with Fluffy Cucumber Sauce (for 8–10)

This is a real treat which requires very little effort. The incongruous marriage of beef and smoked oysters is an inexplicable success. The oysters are mixed with parsley and onion and their smoky flavour permeates the rare roast beef to give an ambrosial taste. The light and refreshing sauce perfects the pleasure of this dish.

105 g can smoked oysters
1 large bunch parsley, finely chopped
1 small onion, finely chopped
black pepper
1 boned rib joint of beef, 3–4 lb
  (1·35–1·80 kg)
olive oil
sea salt

For the sauce
½ cucumber
3 tablespoons plain yogurt
2 teaspoons lemon juice
salt
2–3 pinches cayenne pepper
¼ pint (150 ml) double cream

Put the oysters in a bowl, mix in the chopped parsley and onion, and season with plenty of black pepper. Cut any tight string from the joint of beef and then press the oyster mixture into any cavities. Tie the joint up neatly again with string and rub all over with olive oil. Rub the outside fat with sea salt. Put the meat into a roasting pan and leave for 3–4 hours at room temperature. Then pre-heat the oven to Gas 7/425°F/220°C and cook the beef towards the top of the oven, basting once or twice, for 10–15 minutes a pound (450 g) to give rare beef.

Either beforehand or while the meat is cooking make the sauce. Peel the cucumber and chop finely into small cubes. Put into a bowl and mix in the yogurt and lemon juice. Season with a little salt and cayenne pepper. Whisk the cream until thick and fold gently into the cucumber mixture. Pour into a serving bowl and keep in the fridge until ready to serve with the cooked beef.

Far Eastern Pie (for 6)

This pie has a true flavour of the East with its spicy filling of meat and spinach. It has a creamy topping of ground rice cooked in coconut milk with a golden crunchy crust. If one of your pet hates is cakes and puddings made with coconut please don't be put off; used in this dish the coconut is in no way similar and quite delicious. I serve the pie simply with a salad.

3 oz (75 g) desiccated coconut	1 rounded teaspoon ground
1½ pints (900 ml) milk	cinnamon
1 lb (450 g) fresh spinach	1 level teaspoon ground turmeric
4 cloves garlic	½ teaspoon ground chilli
1 inch (2·5 cm) piece fresh ginger	1½ lb (675 g) minced beef
(optional)	juice of ½ lemon
2 oz (50 g) butter or margarine	1½ oz (40 g) ground rice
2 rounded teaspoon ground	salt
coriander	

Simmer the coconut in the milk for 5 minutes. Then leave the pan on one side while you prepare the rest of the pie. Wash and pick the stalks off the spinach. Plunge the leaves into boiling salted water just for a minute or so until the leaves are limp. Drain well, pressing out the liquid, and chop up roughly. Peel and chop up finely the garlic and the fresh ginger. Heat 1 oz (25 g) of the butter in a large frying pan over a medium heat. Add the ground coriander, cinnamon, turmeric and chilli and stir over the heat for ½ minute. Then add the chopped garlic and ginger and stir for another ½ minute. Add the minced beef and stir over a slightly higher heat for about 5 minutes until brown. Add the chopped spinach. Remove from the heat and stir in the lemon juice. Put the meat mixture into an open, fairly shallow ovenproof dish and put on one side.

To make the topping, put the ground rice in a saucepan and strain in the coconut milk through a sieve, pressing the coconut to extract all the liquid. Leave the coconut on one side for later. Bring the milk and rice to the boil, stirring all the time, and then simmer, stirring a bit, for 5 minutes until cooked and thick. If it seems very thick indeed, stir in a little top of the milk. Season to taste with salt and 2–3 pinches of ground chilli. Pour over and spread on top of the meat mixture. In a small saucepan melt the remaining 1 oz (25 g) of butter. Remove from the heat and stir in the drained coconut. Spoon this mixture evenly over the rice topping. Heat the oven to Gas 5/375°F/190°C. Cook the pie in the centre of the oven for 40–45 minutes until richly browned on top.

Picnic Pie (for 6)

A bread-based pie with tasty mince, onions and carrots topped with bubbling cheese. We gave it its name because it is a satisfying complete meal to take on picnics, wrapped well in foil and layers of newspaper to keep it warm.

1 tablespoon fat
1 onion, chopped into small pieces
2 cloves garlic, finely chopped
8 oz (225 g) minced beef
2 teaspoons paprika
1 level tablespoon tomato purée
1 carrot, grated
salt, black pepper
3 oz (75 g) grated cheese
butter

For the bread base
8 oz (225 g) strong plain flour
1 teaspoon bicarbonate of soda
1 teaspoon cream of tartar
1 teaspoon salt
¼ pint (150 ml) milk

Melt the fat in a large frying pan and fry the chopped onion gently until softened. Add the chopped garlic, turn up the heat a bit and add the minced beef, stirring it round to break it up. Add the paprika, tomato purée and grated carrot. Stir around until the meat is cooked and season well with salt and black pepper. Let the mixture cool.

Meanwhile sift the flour, bicarbonate of soda, cream of tartar and salt into a bowl. Add the milk and mix thoroughly to a softish dough. Using floured hands, gather the dough up and knead lightly. Heat the oven to Gas 6/400°F/200°C. Form the dough into a ball and roll out into a circle a little larger than a 9–10 inch (23–25 cm) greased flan dish. Lay the dough in the flan dish, bringing it up the edges. Spread on the mince mixture and then cover all over with the grated cheese. Dot with butter, and bake in the centre of the oven for about 30 minutes until the bread is risen.

Old English Lattice Pie (for 6)

Using the flavours of seventeenth-century English cooking and a delicious potato pastry, this pie is an easily made and useful lunch or supper dish. I serve it with a good English vegetable such as carrots or cabbage but you could equally well just have a salad. It is also good eaten cold on a picnic.

1 lb (450 g) potatoes
3 oz (75 g) butter
6 oz (175 g) plain flour
1 lb (450 g) minced beef
4 teaspoons horseradish sauce
1 medium onion, finely chopped

2 tablespoons tomato purée
2 oz (50 g) seedless raisins, chopped
¼ whole nutmeg, grated
salt, black pepper
1 tin anchovies

Boil the potatoes in salted water. Then drain and mash smoothly, adding the butter. Sift in the flour and stir in thoroughly with a wooden spoon. Gather up the lump of dough and press over the bottom and up the sides of a 9 inch (23 cm) diameter earthenware flan dish.

Put the minced beef in a bowl together with the horseradish, chopped onion, tomato purée, chopped raisins and grated nutmeg. Season with salt and black pepper and mix well together. Then spoon the mixture into the dough-lined flan dish. Arrange the anchovies in a criss-cross pattern on top, and pour over the oil from the tin. Heat the oven to Gas 6/400°F/200°C and cook the pie in the centre of the oven for 25–30 minutes.

Piglet Pie (for 4–5)

This pie makes a perfect family meal because children adore it. It has a lovely crust of potato pastry (a good way to use up left-over boiled potatoes), and is filled with a tasty mixture of pork, tomatoes and sweetcorn flavoured with mustard and coriander. Serve it either with carrots or a green vegetable, or with a salad.

1 tablespoon sunflower oil
12 oz (350 g) lean minced pork
salt, black pepper
2 teaspoons ground coriander
2 teaspoons French mustard
3–4 tomatoes, chopped fairly small
8 oz (225 g) frozen sweetcorn, boiled
   until tender

For the pastry
4 oz (100 g) plain flour
1 teaspoon baking powder
pinch salt
4 oz (100 g) butter or margarine
6 oz (175 g) cold mashed potato
milk to glaze

Heat the oil in a large frying pan. Season the pork with salt and black pepper and fry it, stirring round with a wooden spoon over a fairly high heat, until sealed. Stir in the coriander, the mustard and the chopped tomatoes and cook more gently, still stirring, for 5 more minutes. Stir in the sweetcorn. Spoon the mixture into a pie plate or a flan dish and leave to cool.

To make the potato pastry sift the flour, baking powder and salt into a bowl. Rub in the butter until the mixture resembles breadcrumbs. Then work in the mashed potato with your hands and knead slightly until you have a smooth dough. Gather into a ball. Roll out the pastry on a floured board into a piece big enough to put over your pie dish. Moisten the edges of the dish. Roll the pastry carefully back over the rolling pin and out again on to the dish. Trim the edges and make cuts round the edge of the pastry with the back of a knife. Roll out the trimmings to make decorations. Heat the oven to Gas 5/375°F/190°C. Brush the pie with milk and cook in the centre of the oven for 25–35 minutes until golden brown all over.

Spiced Pork and Beef Loaf en Croûte

(for 6)

Here is modest mince transformed into an impressive dinner party dish. A succulent pork and cheese mixture sandwiches a centre of mildly spiced beef and vegetables, all wrapped in a golden crust of puff pastry. It is full of flavour and unfailingly popular. Serve with a salad or a crisp green vegetable such as French beans.

For the pork mixture
12 oz (350 g) pork mince
8 oz (225 g) cheese, cut into small cubes
2–3 cloves garlic, finely chopped
2 teaspoons rosemary, finely chopped
1 egg, beaten
salt, black pepper

For the beef mixture
8 oz (225 g) minced beef
3 sticks celery, finely chopped
6 oz (175 g) carrots, grated

1–2 tablespoons tomato purée
1½ teaspoons ground cinnamon
2–3 cloves garlic, finely chopped
1 large egg, beaten
salt, black pepper

For the pastry
13 oz (375 g) packet puff pastry
egg yolk or milk to glaze

For the sauce
1 teaspoon cornflour
a little top of the milk

Mix all the ingredients for the pork mixture together thoroughly, seasoning well with salt and black pepper. In another bowl, mix up all the beef ingredients, again seasoning well. Put a roasting pan half full of water on the centre shelf of the oven and heat the oven to Gas 5/375°F/190°C. Butter a 2 lb (900 g) loaf tin. Spoon half the pork mixture into the tin and smooth level. Then spoon in all the beef mixture and level. Finally top with the remaining pork mixture. Cover with a piece of buttered foil, put the tin into the roasting pan and cook for 1–1¼ hours. When the loaf is cooked, pour the juices from around the meat into a small saucepan and leave on one side. Put the meat in the tin in a cold place to cool.

When the meat is cold, or almost cold, roll out the pastry to a rectangle approximately 10×12 inches (25×30 cm). Trim the edges evenly. Heat the oven to Gas 7/425°F/220°C. Turn the meat out of the tin, place it on the pastry and wrap up like a parcel, moistening the edges to seal. Place in a moist roasting pan with the sealed edges at the bottom. Roll out the trimmings and cut out leaves, etc. for decoration. Moisten their undersides and arrange them on top of the loaf. Cut two small slits to let the steam escape. Brush with egg yolk (for an extra rich glaze) or milk, and bake in the centre of the oven for 20–25 minutes, until golden brown.

To make the sauce, mix the cornflour in a teacup with a little water until smooth and stir it into the reserved meat juices in the saucepan. Bring to the boil, stirring all the time, and bubble for 1 or 2 minutes until thickened. Add a little top of the milk and stir in, then check for seasoning. Serve in a sauce boat with the loaf.

Pork Rissoles Stuffed with Root Fennel

(for 6–7)

In this unusual dish the minced pork is subtly flavoured with orange and leaf fennel while you bite into a tender centre of cooked root fennel. The rissoles are served under a brilliant carrot sauce flavoured with orange juice. The result is extremely good. Serve with new or mashed potatoes and a green salad.

For the rissoles
¾–1 lb (350–450 g) root fennel bulbs
1½ lb (675 g) minced pork
4 oz (100 g) fresh white breadcrumbs
finely grated rind of 1 orange

1 good tablespoon chopped fennel or dill leaves
1 large egg, whisked
salt, black pepper

continued

For the sauce	1 chicken stock cube
13 oz (375 g) carrots	juice of 1 orange
1 pint (600 ml) water	salt, black pepper

Cut any long stalks off the fennel bulbs, reserving any leaves for garnish later. Slice the fennel into ½ inch (1 cm) strips. Steam or boil for a few minutes until tender, then rinse with cold water to cool. In a bowl mix the minced pork with all the other rissole ingredients and season well with salt and black pepper. Divide the cooked fennel into 8 equal piles. Then, using wet hands, divide the meat mixture also into 8 equal piles. Still using wet hands, press a pile of meat out flatly on a wet board. Lay a pile of fennel on top. Bring the meat up round the fennel and form with your hands into a large rissole shape, completely encasing the vegetable. Lay the rissoles in a roasting pan and cover with foil. Heat the oven to Gas 4/350°F/180°C. Cook the rissoles in the centre of the oven for 1 hour, removing the foil for the last 20 minutes to brown them.

While the rissoles are cooking make the carrot sauce. Peel a 1 oz (25 g) piece of carrot, cut it into the thinnest possible little strips and leave on one side. Bring the water to the boil in a saucepan, add the chicken stock cube, and stir to dissolve. Peel and cut up roughly the remaining 12 oz (350 g) of carrots, add to the stock, cover the pan and simmer until soft. Add the orange juice and leave to cool a little.

When the rissoles are cooked, pour the juices off into a saucepan and boil fiercely for 3–4 minutes until reduced to a thick, syrupy sauce. Transfer the rissoles to a serving plate and spoon the syrupy sauce over them. Keep warm in a low oven while you finish the carrot sauce. Whizz the carrots and their stock in a liquidizer until smooth. Then pour into a saucepan, add the reserved carrot strips, re-heat and bubble for 1 minute. Check for seasoning and pour the orange sauce over the rissoles. Sprinkle with the reserved fennel leaves.

Pork, Onions and Mushrooms in Crispy Batter (for 4–5)

This dish is somewhat Chinese in character, but the recipe for the batter came from a Turkish friend who lives in Istanbul. It is made with beer which makes it much lighter and crisper. You can also use it to coat and deep fry pieces of fish, mussels, prawns and raw vegetables too – it is mouth-watering. With this dish serve a simple green salad – I don't think it needs anything else.

12 oz (350 g) belly pork rashers	*For the batter*
1 tablespoon soy sauce	4 oz (100 g) self-raising flour
2–3 pinches cayenne pepper	1 teaspoon salt
2 small onions, finely sliced in rings	1 small egg
3 oz (75 g) mushrooms, sliced	¼ pint (150 ml) beer
oil for deep frying	

Cut the skin off the pork rashers, cut into approximately 1 inch (2·5 cm) squares, and put into a steamer or a sieve suspended over boiling water in a covered saucepan. Steam for 10–15 minutes until the pork is cooked. Put the pork in a bowl and stir in the soy sauce and cayenne. Leave to cool a little. Then add the sliced onions and mushrooms.

To make the batter, sift the flour and salt into a bowl, mix in the egg and gradually add the beer. Beat until smooth, or if possible simply whizz all the ingredients up in a liquidizer or food processor. Heat deep oil in a large frying pan until smoking. Empty the batter into the bowl of pork and vegetables and stir around to coat thoroughly. Fry over a high heat in batches until golden brown, separating pieces as much as possible and draining on absorbent kitchen paper. Pile on a plate and serve immediately.

Pork with Crispy Noodles (for 4)

Children always love crispy noodles, and if you are trying to woo them on to more adventurous tastes a good way to start is with Chinese-style dishes – they always seem to adore spare ribs, for instance. In this recipe, thin tender pieces of pork fillet mixed with fresh ginger and crunchy rings of scarlet and white radishes are piled on to a nest of crispy noodles. (I always try to use groundnut oil for deep frying because it has so little taste or smell.)

4 oz (100 g) Chinese noodles	salt
oil for deep frying	1 rounded tablespoon caster sugar
2 cloves garlic	soy sauce
1 inch (2·5 cm) piece fresh ginger	1 scant tablespoon white wine vinegar
12 oz (350 g) pork fillet	spring onions, chopped, using as
1 bunch radishes	much of the green stalk as possible
1 tablespoon sunflower oil	

Boil the noodles in salted water for 6–8 minutes. Rinse under cold water and drain. Put a large, round, shallow serving dish in a low oven to warm. Heat deep oil in a large frying pan until smoking. Put in the boiled noodles and fry at high heat until golden brown and crisp. Lift out with a slotted spoon and drain on absorbent paper. Spread the noodles in the serving dish and keep warm in a low oven.

Now peel the garlic and ginger and chop up together finely. Slice the pork fillet into very thin slices and slice the radishes finely too. Heat the sunflower oil in a frying pan and fry the garlic and ginger over medium heat for 1 minute. Turn up the heat, add a little more oil if necessary, then add the slices of pork and fry, stirring often, for 5–8 minutes until the pork is cooked. Add a sprinkling of salt, the sugar, a generous sprinkling of soy sauce and the vinegar. Lastly, stir in the radishes and toss around over the heat for a minute. Spoon the pork mixture on to the centre of the crispy noodles and sprinkle with chopped spring onions just before serving.

Nepalese Pork (for 4–5)

This is a mild curry with rich, creamy juices. Serve it with plain long-grain rice and a green vegetable. It does not take long to prepare and makes a good family meal.

1½ lb (675 g) boneless pork	¼ teaspoon chilli powder
3 cloves garlic	1 large green pepper, sliced
2 onions	a little more than ¼ pint (150 ml)
1 oz (25 g) butter or margarine	water
1 teaspoon ground cinnamon	salt
1 teaspoon ground coriander	8 oz (225 g) curd cheese
1 teaspoon turmeric	handful chives, chopped

Cut the meat into largish cubes. Peel the garlic and onions and chop very finely. Heat the oven to Gas 3/325°F/170°C. Melt the butter in an iron casserole. Fry the onions and garlic over medium heat for 2–3 minutes, stirring around. Stir in the dried spices. Add a little more butter if quite dry, then add the meat, and stir around until the meat is sealed all over. Add the sliced pepper and the water. Season with salt. Add the curd cheese and stir round until it has melted. Bring to bubbling, cover, and put in the oven for 1–1½ hours until the meat is tender. Before serving, sprinkle with the chopped chives.

Pork and Salsify with Green Peppercorn Sauce (for 6–7)

Marinating the pork gives it a lovely sharp flavour which contrasts beautifully with the mild salsify and delicate creamy sauce. It is a dish which is popular with everyone.

2 lb (900 g) boneless pork shoulder steaks	**butter**
juice of 1 lemon	**olive or sunflower oil for sautéing**
4–5 tablespoons wine vinegar	**½ pint (300 ml) single cream**
black pepper, salt	**2 level teaspoons green peppercorns, roughly crushed**
2 cloves garlic, crushed	**squeeze lemon juice**
1 lb (450 g) salsify	

Cut the pieces of meat in half and put into the bottom of a non-metallic dish. Mix the lemon juice with the vinegar, the crushed garlic and a generous sprinkling of black pepper and pour over the meat. Cover and leave in the fridge for 8 hours or overnight. Plunge the unpeeled salsify (cut in half if too long) into a pan of boiling water and boil for 8–10 minutes. Drain and peel (it will come off easily) while still warm. Wipe with lemon juice or vinegar to prevent discolouration and leave on one side.

Drain the marinade from the meat. Heat about ½ oz (15 g) butter and a tablespoon of oil in a large frying pan. Fry the meat over a low to medium heat for about 10 minutes on each side until browned. Using a slotted spoon, transfer the meat to an open serving dish and keep warm in a low oven. Heat another 1 oz (25 g) butter in the frying pan. Cut the salsify into approximately 1½ inch (3·5 cm) pieces and sauté for about 5 minutes until browned. Add to the meat, keep warm and don't wash out the frying pan. Just before serving empty the cream into the pan, add the crushed green peppercorns, and season with salt. Bring to bubbling and bubble for about half a minute, stir in a squeeze of lemon juice and pour the sauce over the meat and salsify.

Roast Pickled Pork (for 8 or more)

From time to time, usually during the school holidays when I have to feed a lot of people satisfying meals which don't need too much preparation, I experiment with salting pork, beef and even sausages in a brine jar. By experiment I mean I try out all sorts of different combinations of spices and herbs to flavour the meat. It is always more delicious than when it is done by the butcher, and the meat is good either hot or cold. If you mean to eat the meat cold only, I like to cut off the rind (which makes crackling when it is hot) before putting the meat in the brine.

Here is a recipe for hot pickled pork. If you like it, use it as a guide for future pickling and try out different flavours. If you use good sausages with a high proportion of meat they become something much more subtle and interesting. You can add a mixture of Indian spices, a tablespoon of chilli powder and quite a lot of roughly chopped garlic to the brine and you will get sausages with an exotic and piquant flavour. Needless to say, a large piece of meat (you may have to increase the amount of brine for this) of say 6–8 lb (2·70–3·60 kg) boned weight should stay in the brine for 8–12 days, a 4–5 lb (1·80–2·25 kg) piece as in this recipe for 5–7 days, while sausages can be used after 3–4 days. An extra large joint could have another teaspoon of saltpetre added to the brine, but too much saltpetre toughens the meat. Don't be put off if the brine looks cloudy and unappetizing and in warm weather has mould on it – this is of no consequence and all in a delicious cause!

When you have once prepared a brine you will realize that the preparation is almost quicker to do than to write out, and the subtle flavour of pickled meat makes it a most satisfying operation.

4–5 lb (1·80–2·25 kg) piece of boned pork (a cheaper joint such as hand and spring is best)

For the brine
4 oz (100 g) sea salt
6 oz (175 g) brown sugar
4 pints (2·3 litres) water
15–20 juniper berries
2 teaspoons coriander seeds
2 teaspoons black peppercorns

} roughly crushed

2 pieces stick cinnamon, broken in half
3 bay leaves
2–3 sprigs rosemary or thyme
1 level teaspoon saltpetre (available from most chemists)

Get the butcher to bone and roll the pork neatly and score the fat evenly. (I often do it myself in a diamond pattern, which looks effective.)

To make the brine, dissolve the salt and sugar in 4 pints (2·3 litres) very hot water in a saucepan. Then stir in the spices and herbs (but not the saltpetre). Bring to the boil and simmer for about 5 minutes. Then cover and allow the brine to become completely cold, leaving it overnight if you like. When it is quite cold stir in the saltpetre. Then lay the meat in a glazed earthenware or glass dish into which it fits quite snugly. Strain the brine over the meat and cover with a lid or foil. Leave in a cool place (the fridge is not necessary) for 6–7 days, but turn the meat now and then to ensure even pickling.

Before cooking, rinse the meat under a cold tap (but don't soak it) and put it into a saucepan with enough water to cover and a roughly sliced onion and carrot. Bring only just to the boil, and simmer very gently for 30 minutes. Drain and dry the meat, and roast either at once or next day if you like. To roast, rub the meat all over with oil, sprinkle the rind with salt and lay in a roasting pan rind side upwards. Heat the oven to Gas 7/425°F/220°C and roast for 35–45 minutes, basting occasionally.

Roast Pork with Apple and Walnut Stuffing (for 8–10)

Taking the trouble to stuff an inexpensive pork joint such as hand, blade bone or even a large piece of belly can transform it into a dish fit for a gourmet.

2½–3½ lb (1·25–1·50 kg) boned joint of pork	1 small egg, whisked
1 large cooking apple	salt, black pepper
squeeze lemon juice	2 cloves garlic, crushed
1 tablespoon sugar	oil
2 oz (50 g) fresh brown breadcrumbs	½ pint (300 ml) beer
2 oz (50 g) walnuts, chopped	1 teaspoon arrowroot or cornflour

If the boned joint has been rolled up, undo the string and lay the piece of meat out flat. Peel and grate the apple and put it in a mixing bowl, stirring in a little lemon juice at the same time. Stir in the sugar, breadcrumbs, walnuts, egg and seasoning in that order. Spread the garlic over the meat and spoon the stuffing on to it or into any pockets in the meat (this will depend on how it has been boned). Roll the meat up round the stuffing and fasten with string or skewers. Smear the joint all over with oil, score the thick skin well with a sharp knife if not already done, and rub with coarse salt to make good, crisp crackling.

Heat the oven to Gas 8/450°F/230°C. Put the joint in a roasting pan towards the top of the oven for 20 minutes, then move it to the centre of the oven and turn the heat down to Gas 4/350°F/180°C for another 2–2½ hours, basting occasionally. When 30–45 minutes of the cooking time are left, tip out the fat and pour the beer into the roasting pan. This will produce the most delicious gravy. When you have removed the joint, thicken the gravy with the arrowroot or cornflour dissolved in a little water and bubbled up with the juices in the pan.

Pork Steaks with Apple and Spring Onions (for 4)

This is very simple but good enough for any occasion. It is, of course, a new version of an old combination of flavours. Baby carrots and new potatoes are excellent with this dish.

4 boneless pork shoulder steaks or spare rib chops, 1–1½ lb (450–675 g)
1–2 cloves garlic, crushed
salt, black pepper
1 dessertspoon chopped fresh rosemary
2–3 oz (50–75 g) butter or margarine

4 oz (100 g) mushrooms, finely sliced
1 firm eating apple, thinly sliced
1 bunch spring onions, chopped small, using as much of the green stalk as possible
1 wineglass apple juice or sweet cider

Rub the pork steaks with the crushed garlic, sprinkle with salt and pepper and pat on the rosemary. Fry gently in about 1 oz (25 g) of butter, turning once, for 8–10 minutes on each side. Then transfer to a serving dish and keep warm in the oven. Add another 1 oz (25 g) butter to the pan juices and toss the sliced mushrooms, apple and spring onions over a medium heat for about 2 minutes – not more. Spoon the mixture over the steaks. Then pour the apple juice, seasoned with salt and pepper, into the pan and bubble fiercely over a strong heat for 2–3 minutes, until the juice has slightly thickened. Pour this sauce over the steaks.

Roman Cobbler (for 4–5)

In our family this recipe is more popular than Shepherd's Pie, which is saying a lot, and it is not much trouble to make. The golden top is a cheesy Italian gnocchi mixture, and the pork underneath is particularly tasty.

For the topping
¼ whole nutmeg, grated
1 pint (600 ml) milk
salt, black pepper
4 oz (100 g) fine semolina
3 oz (75 g) grated cheese
1 oz (25 g) butter or margarine
1 egg, lightly whisked

For the filling
1¼–1½ lb (550–675 g) boneless pork shoulder steaks

salt, black pepper
1 oz (25 g) butter or margarine, plus a little more
1 tablespoon oil
2–3 cloves garlic, finely chopped
small handful fresh sage leaves, finely chopped
4 oz (100 g) mushrooms, sliced
grated Parmesan cheese

Make the topping at least 2 hours in advance, as follows. Add the nutmeg to the milk in a saucepan, together with salt and black pepper. Stir in the semolina. Bring the milk to the boil and simmer gently for 3–4 minutes until very thick, stirring all the time. Remove from the heat and add the grated cheese, the butter and the whisked egg. Return to a low heat and stir for a minute more. Oil a large Swiss roll tin or roasting pan. Spread the mixture evenly over the bottom of the tin. Cover with a cloth and leave to get completely cold – in the fridge if possible.

Using a sharp knife, cut the pork into very small pieces and season with salt and black pepper. Melt 1 oz (25 g) butter and the oil in a large frying pan. Stir the pork pieces and chopped garlic over a medium heat for about 5 minutes, until cooked. Add the sage and mushrooms and cook for a further minute or two, stirring the mixture. Transfer the meat and mushrooms with a slotted spoon to a shallow, ovenproof dish. Bubble the remaining liquid in the pan over a strong heat for a moment or so, until reduced and slightly thickened, and pour over the meat.

Set the grill on medium heat, cut the cooled topping mixture into fingers about 2×1 inches (5×2·5 cm), and arrange in an overlapping pattern all over the meat. Dot with butter, sprinkle generously with grated Parmesan, and put under the grill until a rich, golden brown. If necessary, keep the dish hot until needed in a very low oven.

Ham Rolls Stuffed with Turkey Breast, with Spinach Sauce (for 4)

This is a simple, pretty and delectable dish. When I made it for the first time my elder daughter said, 'Oh please, give me more and more.' The delicate flavours mingle beautifully together. Serve it with new potatoes if possible, and baby carrots too.

12 oz (350 g) skinned turkey breast fillets	salt, pepper
4 oz (100 g) curd cheese	8 oblong slices ham
1 large egg yolk	butter or margarine
1 medium bunch fresh chives	1 lb (450 g) spinach, roughly chopped

Either mince the turkey fillets or chop them up in a food processor. Mix them thoroughly in a bowl with the curd cheese and egg yolk. Chop the chives finely (I hold the bunch and snip with scissors) and stir them into the mixture. Season with salt and pepper.

Lay out the slices of ham, and spoon the mixture evenly towards the end of each piece. Roll each up lengthwise and arrange the rolls closely together in an ovenproof dish. Smear them with some softened butter. Cover the dish with foil. Put a large pan or dish half full of water in the oven just below the centre and heat the oven to Gas 4/350°F/180°C. Then put the dish in the pan of water and cook for 1 hour. Pour the juices surrounding the rolls into a large saucepan. Keep the rolls warm, covered with foil. Cook the spinach in the juices, with the pan covered, until tender. Season with pepper, then purée in a liquidizer or food processor until smooth. If the purée seems very thick (some types of spinach reduce more than others) add some butter. Spoon the purée roughly over the rolls just before serving.

Pork and Chicken Slivers with Parmesan Meringue (for 5–6)

This dish is quite sophisticated enough for an adult meal, but children love the delicate flavour and texture too. The tender pieces of pork fillet, chicken breast and sweet onion are wrapped in a tasty sauce rich with egg yolks and topped with a golden Parmesan meringue.

¾–1 lb (350–450 g) pork fillet
8 oz (225 g) chicken breast fillets, skinned
salt, black pepper
approx. 1 oz (25 g) butter
2 large onions, peeled and sliced in rings

1 level tablespoon caster sugar
1 level tablespoon cornflour
¾ pint (450 ml) milk
3 large eggs, separated
2 tablespoons white wine vinegar
2 oz (50 g) grated Parmesan cheese

Using a sharp knife, cut the pork fillet fairly thinly across into small slices. Lay the slices spaced out on a large sheet of oiled greaseproof paper. Put another sheet of paper on top and bash evenly with a rolling pin until the slices are thin and spread out. Do the same thing with slices of the chicken breast. Sprinkle both the pork and chicken with salt and black pepper. Heat the butter in a large frying pan and fry the pieces of meat and chicken over a medium heat for 2–3 minutes on each side until cooked – you will have to do this in relays but it does not take long. Add more butter if necessary. Transfer to a fairly large shallow ovenproof dish and put on one side. Melt some more butter in the pan and fry the onion rings gently, turning around often until soft. Thoroughly stir the caster sugar into the pan and then mix the onions with the meat and chicken in the dish.

In a saucepan mix the cornflour with a tablespoon of the milk until smooth and then add the remaining milk. Put over the heat and bring to the boil, stirring. Then allow to bubble for 2 minutes, still stirring. Remove from the heat and whisk the egg yolks into the sauce (putting the whites into a large bowl on one side). Put the sauce back on a low heat and stir constantly for 2 minutes without allowing to boil. Gradually add the wine vinegar and season with salt and black pepper. Pour the sauce over the meat and onions.

Heat the oven to Gas 5/375°F/190°C. Whisk the egg whites into soft peaks and gently fold in about three-quarters of the Parmesan. Spoon the mixture over the sauce-covered meat, and sprinkle the remaining Parmesan on top. Put in the centre of the oven for 15–20 minutes until golden brown. (The dish will keep warm in a low oven for half an hour or so if necessary.)

Veal Stuffed Pork Rolls with Lemon and Parsley Sauce (for 5–6)

These tender little rolls are mouth-watering. The pork fillets are flattened until very thin and then wrapped around a stuffing of minced veal and tomato flavoured with coriander and garlic. It's a dish which is equally suitable for a family meal or for a dinner party. Serve with new potatoes or rice and young carrots.

1 tablespoon olive oil	salt, black pepper
1 medium onion, chopped	4–6 pinches of cayenne pepper
2–3 cloves garlic, finely chopped	12 oz (350 g) pork fillet
2 rounded teaspoons ground coriander	1 egg, beaten
	½ pint (300 ml) water
12 oz (350 g) veal or lamb mince	juice of 1 lemon
2 medium tomatoes, skinned and chopped small	2 teaspoons cornflour
	handful parsley, finely chopped

Heat the oil in a large frying pan, and fry the onion gently until soft. Then add the garlic and coriander and stir for ½ minute. Increase the heat, add the mince and fry, stirring and breaking up with a wooden spoon, until cooked. Lower the heat again and add the tomatoes. Cook, stirring, until the tomatoes are soft and the mixture dry. Season with salt and cayenne pepper, to taste. Remove from the heat and leave on one side.

Cut the pork fillet across into ½ inch (1 cm) slices. Lay the slices, well spaced out, on a large sheet of oiled greaseproof paper. Cover with another sheet of oiled paper. Beat out evenly with a rolling pin (not too hard or the meat will break up) until the pieces are thin and two to three times their original size. Mix the beaten egg into the mince mixture and then spoon the mixture across the middle of each thin piece of pork. Roll the meat up round the mince filling and place the rolls in a roasting pan, join side down. Press any mince that falls out back into the rolls. Heat the oven to Gas 4/350°F/180°C. Pour the water into the roasting pan and cover with foil. Cook in the centre of the oven for 45 minutes.

Using a slotted spatula, transfer the rolls, when cooked, to a serving dish. Strain the juices into a saucepan and add the lemon juice. Mix the cornflour with 2 tablespoons of water until smooth and then stir into the stock and lemon juice. Bring to the boil, stirring, and allow to bubble, still stirring, for 2–3 minutes. Season to taste with salt and black pepper, stir in the chopped parsley and pour over the pork rolls before serving.

Veal with Peppers and Avocado (for 5–6)

The rich flavour of hot avocado blends well in this pretty dish of grilled veal and peppers. It goes well with new potatoes and a green salad or vegetable.

2 yellow or red peppers, or one of each	1 teaspoon ground coriander
1½–2 lb (675–900 g) shoulder of veal	1 large ripe avocado
olive oil	white wine vinegar
salt, black pepper	1 bunch spring onions, finely chopped

First cut the peppers in half lengthwise. Take out the seeds and lay skin side up under a very hot grill until the skin is blackened. Pick the peel off under cold water and then slice into fairly thin strips. Cut the veal into thin strips about 1 inch (2·5 cm) wide and 3–4 inches (7·5–10 cm) long. Lay these pieces of veal well apart on a sheet of oiled greaseproof paper. Lay another sheet of oiled greaseproof paper on top. Bang out with a rolling pin until the pieces of veal are very thin and enlarged. Smear all over with olive oil and season with salt and black pepper. Lay the pieces of veal on the grill (you will probably have to do this in two batches unless you have a very large grill) and cook under a high heat for about 5 minutes on each side. Transfer the meat to a serving dish and put to keep warm in a low oven, pouring the juices off into a large frying pan.

Shortly before eating, heat the juices to bubbling and add the ground coriander. Turn down the heat and add the strips of pepper. Cut the avocado in half, carefully peel off the skin, and slice the halves across into thin half-moon shapes. Sprinkle with white wine vinegar to prevent discolouration and add to the pan. Stir over the heat for about 1 minute and lastly stir in the chopped spring onions. Season with a little salt and black pepper, spoon the mixture over the grilled veal, and serve.

Veal and Tuna Croquettes with Creamy Caper Sauce (for 4)

The Italians are familiar with the combination of veal and tuna in a delicious cold dish called Vitello Tonnato. These hot croquettes are extremely simple to make and I think equally tasty. New potatoes and either broccoli, broad beans or French beans go well with the sauce.

12 oz (350 g) minced veal
7 oz (200 g) can tuna fish
1–2 cloves garlic, crushed
1 sprig rosemary, finely chopped
salt, black pepper
1 large egg, whisked
1 teaspoon green peppercorns
 (optional)

1 oz (25 g) butter
½ pint (300 ml) single cream
2 rounded teaspoons capers, roughly
 crushed
a little parsley to garnish

In a mixing bowl put the veal, the tuna fish with its juices, the crushed garlic and the chopped rosemary. Season with salt and black pepper. Very thoroughly pound and mix together well with a large wooden spoon. Then mix in the whisked egg and the green peppercorns if used. Using wet hands, form the mixture into small, short sausage shapes. Heat the butter in a large frying pan and cook the croquettes over a medium heat for about 5 minutes on each side, turning carefully until golden brown. Remove the croquettes with a slotted spoon and put into a heated serving dish.

Pour off the fat from the pan, pour in the cream and heat to just bubbling, stir in the crushed capers and season with salt and pepper, just allowing to bubble for ½ minute. Then pour the sauce over the croquettes, garnish with a little chopped parsley and serve.

Aubergines Stuffed with Lamb and Almonds (for 4)

I always think these look like heavily laden cargo boats sailing on a red sunset sea. Variations of stuffed aubergines dominate Middle Eastern cookery, particularly in Turkey. They are usually served cold as a first course. However, in this recipe they make an excellent hot main course, served with plain long grain rice to mop up the juices, and a salad. If you prefer a vegetable, broad beans go well.

2 large aubergines, weighing 8–12 oz
  (225–350 g) each
2 large onions, peeled and chopped
1 lb (450 g) minced lamb
1 heaped teaspoon cumin
1 heaped teaspoon cinnamon
2 teaspoons paprika

2–3 large cloves garlic, finely chopped
2 oz (50 g) flaked almonds
salt, black pepper
2–3 tablespoons tomato purée
juice of 1 lemon
4–5 tablespoons olive or sunflower oil
4 tablespoons plain yogurt

Cut the stalks off the aubergines and slice them in half lengthways. Scoop out about half of the flesh, making the aubergines into a boat shape. Soak both the scooped-out flesh and the shells in a bowl of strongly salted water for at least 30 minutes – this removes the bitter juices. Fry the onions gently in a little oil until becoming soft. Add the lamb and stir over the heat until browned. Stir in the spices, the garlic and the almonds and the scooped-out aubergine flesh, chopped into small pieces. Season with salt and black pepper and remove from the heat.

Heat the oven to Gas 7/425°F/220°C. Lay the aubergine shells in an open ovenproof dish. Spoon in the minced meat filling, pressing it in and piling it up. Mix the tomato purée with a little water and pour it into the dish, then add enough water to come to quarter to half-way up the aubergines. Add the lemon juice and spoon the oil over the aubergines. Bake uncovered at Gas 7/425°F/220°C for 15–20 minutes, then lower the heat to Gas 2/300°F/150°C for about 1¼ hours, basting occasionally with the juices, until the aubergines' shells are completely soft when you stick a sharp knife in them. Before serving spoon the yogurt over each aubergine boat. This dish can be prepared and cooked well beforehand and kept warm in a low oven.

Lamb Burgers, Middle Eastern Style

(for 4)

Here is a more substantial and exotic sandwich which my children love. This tasty lamb stuffed into flat pitta breads makes a satisfying all-in-one light meal.

1 lb (450 g) minced lamb	1 egg, beaten
3 cloves garlic, finely chopped	salt, black pepper
1 tablespoon wholewheat flour	4 flat pitta breads
2 level teaspoons ground cumin	handful fresh mint
3 level teaspoons ground coriander	1 small onion
2 level teaspoons ground cinnamon	lemon wedges

If possible, grind the minced lamb up finely in a food processor or put through a mincer twice more. Put into a bowl and add the chopped garlic, the flour, the spices, the egg and a generous seasoning of salt and black pepper. Mix all together thoroughly with a wooden spoon. Spread the mixture out on a large baking sheet (this has to go under the grill, so if you have a small grill you may have to do the meat in two halves, using a smaller baking sheet). Press the meat down with your hands to make a thin even layer all over the baking sheet. Wrap the pitta breads in foil and heat in a moderate oven. Chop up the mint leaves fairly roughly and slice the onion in the finest possible rings.

Heat the grill. Put the meat under the hot grill for about 5 minutes until browned and somewhat shrunken, then turn the meat over using a wide spatula and your hands. Grill the second side for another 4–5 minutes. Then cut the meat into thin strips. Using a sharp knife, cut the pitta breads down one side using your hands to open them up like a pocket. Stuff each bread with pieces of the meat and chopped mint and sliced onion. Squeeze lemon juice over the meat before eating.

Golden Hearted Lamb in Pastry (for 6–8)

This is a beautiful, mouth-watering dish of aromatic lamb wrapped in crumbling pastry with a bright orange stuffing of carrots. You cook the meat first and then let it cool, so you must start well in advance, but although it looks so impressive it is a straightforward and failsafe recipe.

For the pastry	olive oil
12 oz (350 g) plain flour	juice of 1 lemon
pinch salt	1 large clove garlic, crushed
6 oz (175 g) butter	salt, black pepper
2 oz (50 g) lard	about 1 tablespoon thyme or oregano
2 eggs, whisked	handful fresh mint leaves (if available)
	12 oz (350 g) large carrots, topped
a 4–5 lb (1·80–2·25 kg) shoulder of	and tailed and boiled whole
lamb, boned by the butcher but not	1 egg yolk
rolled	

Rub the lamb with olive oil and lemon juice, and leave at room temperature for 1 hour or more if possible. Meanwhile make the pastry by cutting the fat into the flour and salt and crumbling the mixture with your fingertips until it looks like breadcrumbs. Then stir in the whisked eggs and a little very cold water with a round bladed knife until the mixture just begins to stick together. Gather into a ball, wrap in polythene, and cool in the fridge.

Lay the lamb out skin side down and rub crushed garlic all over the meat. Sprinkle with salt, black pepper and the herbs and lay the mint leaves all over if you have them. Then lay the carrots in the centre lengthways and roll the meat round them, trying to make a neat parcel and using tightly tied string and skewers if it helps. (It doesn't matter how much string or how many skewers you use as they are removed before the pastry stage.) Rub the lamb parcel with a little oil or fat and roast in a pre-heated oven at Gas 3/325°F/170°C, basting occasionally, for about 2 hours. Remove from the oven, put the lamb on a plate to cool, and reserve the juices in a bowl. When the lamb is quite cold carefully cut away all the string and take out any skewers.

Heat the oven to Gas 6/400°F/200°C. Roll out the pastry and wrap it round the piece of meat, dampening the edges and pressing lightly to seal them. Roll out the trimmings and cut out some decorations, moisten them, and arrange them on the pastry parcel. I usually try to do a cut-out lamb and a large carrot for this, but you could just do leaves if you don't feel inspired! Mix the egg yolk with a tiny spot of milk and brush all over the pastry to produce a golden professional-looking shine. Cook in the centre of the oven for 25–35 minutes. Bubble up the reserved lamb juices with a glass of vermouth or dry sherry and serve as a gravy.

Anchovy Lamb Stuffed with Mint and Cucumber (for 8–10)

The combination of anchovies with lamb was a Victorian favourite which in my opinion should never have been forgotten. It does not result in a fishy flavour at all, but something much more subtle. Here a boned shoulder of anchovy-flavoured lamb is wrapped round a whole cucumber, which gives a refreshing and surprising soft green centre.

a 3½–4½ lb (1·50–2·00 kg) shoulder
  of lamb, boned but not rolled
large handful fresh mint leaves
2 cloves garlic
1 tin anchovies

salt, black pepper
1 short cucumber
1 glass vermouth or white wine
1 carton soured cream

Lay the lamb out flat. Chop the mint and garlic finely together. Slice the anchovies into tiny pieces and mix with the mint and garlic, moistening with the oil from the anchovy tin. Season with salt and black pepper. Spread the mixture all over the meat. Then peel the cucumber and roll it up in the middle of the meat. If possible, turn the ends of the meat in to overlap the cucumber completely. Tie up with pieces of string to secure neatly. Rub with salt and some oil and put in a roasting pan. Heat the oven to Gas 3/325°F/170°C. Cook in the oven for 2–2½ hours, pouring off the fat and adding a glass of vermouth to the juices half an hour before the end. Before serving snip off the bits of string. Stir the soured cream into the pan juices and use as a sauce.

Marinated Lamb Fillets with Sesame and Coriander Seeds (for 4–6)

Tender lamb fillets only appear in the butchers at certain times of the year, but make the most of them when they do. This recipe is very simple but always tastes like a subtle and unusual treat. It's important that the centre of the lamb should still be pink, so don't overcook. I would serve the dish with new or sauté potatoes and with minty fresh peas if they are in season.

2 tablespoons sesame oil
juice of 1 lemon
2 rounded tablespoons sesame seeds
3 teaspoons coriander seeds, crushed
  finely
2–3 cloves garlic, crushed
3–4 pinches cayenne pepper

4 lamb fillets, approx. 6–8 oz
  (175–225 g) each
salt
to decorate – large mint or lettuce
  leaves and a few chopped coriander
  or parsley leaves

Mix the sesame oil, lemon juice, sesame seeds, crushed coriander seeds, crushed garlic and cayenne pepper together. Rub this mixture on the lamb fillets and lay them in a roasting pan, covered with a piece of foil. Leave the pan in a cool place, rubbing the lamb fillets again with the marinade now and again, for several hours or overnight. Then heat the oven to Gas 9/475°F/240°C, remove the foil from the pan and cook the lamb at the very top of the oven for 15–20 minutes.

Before serving, cut the lamb crossways into thin slices, using a very sharp knife. Lay the pieces overlapping neatly on a flat serving dish, decorated round the edge with mint and/or lettuce leaves. Sprinkle the meat with a little salt and pour over the juices from the pan. Finally scatter over a few chopped coriander or parsley leaves.

Lamb and Leeks with Green Velvet Sauce (for 4)

Lamb neck fillets are tender and succulent. Here they are cooked with leeks and cumin. The sauce is made in the new way without using flour or eggs to thicken it, and it is light and particularly delicious. It is also excellent with fish and veal.

For the sauce
2 tablespoons olive oil
1 tablespoon lemon juice
4 tablespoons water
1 large green pepper ⎤
1 large onion   ⎥ roughly
3–4 cloves garlic   ⎦ sliced
salt, black pepper

1¼–1½ lb (550–675 g) lamb neck
  fillets
3–4 leeks
2 tablespoons olive or sunflower oil
2 rounded teaspoons ground cumin
salt, black pepper
chopped fresh mint or parsley to
  garnish

Put the sauce ingredients together into a saucepan. Cover the pan, put over the heat and simmer gently for 15–20 minutes until everything is completely soft. Meanwhile cut the lamb fillets crossways into ¾ inch (1·5 cm) slices. Slice the leeks into thin rings. Heat the oil in a large frying pan and sauté the lamb and leeks over a gentle heat, stirring often, until the leeks are soft – about 15–25 minutes. Then stir in the cumin, salt and pepper and cook for a minute more. Transfer to a warmed serving dish.

Now put the cooked pepper and onion mixture into a liquidizer or food processor and whizz until smooth. Spoon this thickish sauce over the lamb. If necessary, cover the dish with foil and keep warm in a very low oven until ready to eat. Just before serving, sprinkle a few chopped mint or parsley leaves over the top.

Manti with Fresh Tomato Sauce (for 6–8)

You may think that this must be a first cousin of Italian ravioli but, in fact, it is an ancient Mongolian dish which is also found in Turkey. It takes time to make all the little manti but it is quite fun and much quicker if you can get one of your children or a friend to do it with you. In any case, it is a dish which can be prepared ahead and either kept warm or reheated. With the buttery tomato sauce it is absolutely delicious. Serve it simply with a green salad.

For the manti
8 oz (225 g) plain flour
1 teaspoon salt
1 egg, beaten
4–5 tablespoons water
12 oz (350 g) lamb or veal mince
1 medium onion, grated
handful parsley, finely chopped
salt, black pepper

For the tomato sauce
1 lb (450 g) tomatoes
2 oz (50 g) butter
1 clove garlic, crushed
1 tablespoon chopped fresh basil or parsley
salt, black pepper

Sift the flour and salt into a bowl. Make a well in the middle and add the beaten egg. Stir with a wooden spoon and add just enough water to form a dough. Gather the dough up with floured hands and knead well on a floured surface for 5–10 minutes, until smooth and pliable. Cover with cling film and leave on one side. Put the lamb or veal in a bowl and add the onion and parsley. Season well with salt and black pepper and mix together thoroughly.

Roll out the dough on a large, well-floured surface as thinly as you possibly can without tearing it. Then, using a sharp knife, cut it into 1½–2 inch (3·5–5 cm) squares. Place a small teaspoon of the meat mixture into the centre of each square, moisten the edges, and fold over corner to corner to make little triangles, pinching the edges to seal. As you finish the triangles lay them on one side. Re-roll any leftover strips of dough. When all the manti are made, bring a very large pan of salted water to the boil. Put in the manti, cover the pan, and simmer gently for 15 minutes. Lift out carefully with a slotted spoon and put into a colander. Rinse through briefly with hot water and then turn into a large earthenware dish. Cover with foil and put in a low oven to keep warm while you make the sauce.

Pour boiling water over the tomatoes in a bowl. Leave for ½ minute and then drain and skin. Slice up roughly. Heat the butter in a frying pan and add the chopped tomatoes and the garlic. Simmer very gently, stirring once or twice, for 10–15 minutes, until the tomatoes are quite soft and mushy. Then stir in the basil or parsley and season to taste with salt and black pepper. Pour the sauce over the manti and serve.

Crystal Chicken

This Chinese way of cooking a chicken to eat cold is unbelievably effortless and produces a pure white bird of perfect texture and delicate flavour which carves easily into thin, moist slices. It is perfect for summer meals and picnics. You simply stick metal skewers through the chicken – these act as heat conductors and it actually cooks by just sitting in water which has been brought to the boil for a moment only. There can be no more gentle or fuel-saving method of cooking.

a 3–3½ lb (1·35–1·50 kg) fresh
  roasting chicken
just over 3 tablespoons white wine
  vinegar

1 onion, peeled and roughly sliced
3–4 slices fresh ginger
1 bunch spring onions, chopped
soy sauce

Rub the chicken all over with a little vinegar and insert four metal skewers through the body and legs. Put enough water to cover the chicken into a large heavy saucepan – but don't put in the chicken yet. Add the 3 tablespoons of vinegar to the water and bring to a fast boil. Put in the onion, the ginger and the chicken and bring to the boil again for ½ minute. Cover the pan and turn off the heat. Leave the chicken in the water until it gets completely cold. Then chill the drained chicken in the fridge. To serve, carve in very thin slices and arrange on a dish. Scatter with chopped spring onions, and just before serving sprinkle streaks of soy sauce over the chicken.

Grilled Chicken
Marinated with Indian Spices (for 4–6)

The taste of these tender, marinated pieces of chicken is sublime. Children love them, everyone loves them, they are always a success. They are simple to prepare, just as good hot or cold, and perfect for picnics. They are ideal for a barbecue. If you have them as a hot meal, serve them with rice (nutty basmati rice if possible) accompanied by a bowl of yogurt and mint and a vegetable. If eating cold serve salads with them. If you don't have all the spices, don't worry, simply add a little more of the ones you do have.

2–2½ lb (900–1·25 kg) small chicken pieces (drumsticks or larger joints cut in half) or 1¼–1½ lb (550–675 g) boneless chicken

For the marinade
1 small onion, roughly sliced
1 inch (2·5 cm) piece fresh ginger, peeled and roughly chopped
6–8 cloves garlic, peeled

3 teaspoons ground coriander
2 teaspoons ground cumin
2 teaspoons ground cinnamon
1 teaspoon ground cardamom
½ teaspoon ground cloves
½ teaspoon cayenne pepper
3 tablespoons red wine vinegar
3 tablespoons sunflower oil
1 tablespoon tomato purée
1 rounded teaspoon salt

Remove any skin from the pieces of chicken. If using boneless chicken, slice it into fairly thin strips. Put all the marinade ingredients into a liquidizer and whizz to a smooth paste. Put the chicken pieces into a dish or bowl, spoon in the marinade paste and mix very thoroughly all over the chicken, rubbing in a bit. Cover the bowl and leave in a cool place or the fridge for 4 hours or more, overnight if convenient.

Heat the grill to the highest heat. Spread the chicken pieces on a baking sheet (you may have to cook them in two batches if your grill is small), and grill for 8–15 minutes on each side (according to the size of the chicken pieces) until almost black in patches.

Marbles of Chicken Breast with Lemon and Cardamom (for 4–5)

These little balls have a wonderfully delicate flavour and colour. They are easy to make and always a great success, particularly as a light summer meal accompanied by a salad and some new potatoes.

12 oz (350 g) chicken breast fillets, skinned
2 oz (50 g) fresh white breadcrumbs
¾ bunch spring onions, finely chopped
finely grated rind of 1 lemon
8–10 cardamom pods

1 egg, whisked
3–4 pinches cayenne pepper
salt
butter
sunflower oil
1 carton soured cream
a little chopped parsley to garnish

Chop the chicken breast fillets in a food processor, or mince them. Put into a bowl and mix with the breadcrumbs, the chopped spring onions and the lemon rind. Pop the seeds out of the cardamom pods and crush them finely. Add them to the chicken mixture together with the whisked egg, the cayenne pepper and salt. Using wet hands, form into small balls the size of large marbles. Heat a good knob of butter and a tablespoon of sunflower oil in a frying pan, add the chicken balls, and fry over a fairly gentle heat for about 15 minutes, turning around several times to cook evenly. Transfer to a warm serving dish and if necessary keep warm in a low oven. Then heat the soured cream in a saucepan and spoon over the balls. Sprinkle with chopped parsley and serve.

Chicken Balls Kiev (for 4–5)

These resemble a tiny version of Chicken Kiev but they are made with minced chicken, poached and served with a cream and egg yolk sauce instead of being coated in breadcrumbs and fried. However, in the same irresistible way, they burst forth with liquid butter as you cut them open. Serve with a green vegetable such as broccoli, broad beans or petits pois, and with new potatoes or egg noodles.

12 oz (350 g) chicken breast fillets, skinned	1½–2 oz (40–50 g) butter, cold from the fridge
3 oz (75 g) fresh white breadcrumbs	5 fl oz (150 ml) carton soured cream
2–3 cloves garlic, crushed	1 tablespoon single cream or top of the milk
salt, black pepper	
2 eggs, separated	1 tablespoon chopped fresh tarragon

Mince the chicken fillets or chop them in a food processor. Put in a bowl with the breadcrumbs and garlic and season with plenty of salt and black pepper. Add the unbeaten egg whites and work in thoroughly with a wooden spoon. With damp hands, form the mixture into balls the size of large marbles. Then cut off little squares of butter, form a hole in each ball, insert the butter and press the mixture round again to enclose it. Bring a large pan of water to the boil, drop in the chicken balls, and continue boiling vigorously for a few minutes until all the balls rise to the top. Lift them out with a slotted spoon and put closely together in a shallow ovenproof dish. Cover with foil and keep warm in a low oven while making the sauce.

Before serving, put the egg yolks, soured cream, single cream or top of the milk and tarragon in a small saucepan with salt and black pepper. Heat very gently, stirring, not allowing to bubble, for a few minutes until the sauce thickens a little. Pour over the chicken balls and serve.

Chicken Baked with Honey and Ginger

(for 6)

This is an extremely easy and useful dish with delicious sweet and sour juices. If you cannot get fresh ginger, crystallized ginger will do. Any joints of chicken can be used.

6 joints chicken
2 tablespoons vegetable oil
handful fresh mint, chopped
2 teaspoons fresh or dried rosemary
2 cloves garlic, chopped
1–1½ inch (2·5–3·5 cm) piece fresh
  root ginger, peeled and finely
  chopped

1 dessertspoon candied peel
salt, black pepper
4–6 oz (100–175 g) mushrooms, sliced
generous sprinkling soy sauce
1 tablespoon honey
1 tablespoon olive oil

Heat the oven to Gas 4/350°F/180°C. Fry the chicken joints in the vegetable oil until golden and place them in a large, fairly shallow, ovenproof dish. Sprinkle the mint, rosemary, garlic, ginger, peel, salt and black pepper on both sides of the chicken. Arrange the mushrooms both underneath and above the joints. Sprinkle on the soy sauce and spoon over the honey and olive oil. Cover the dish with foil or a lid, and cook in the oven for 1¼–1½ hours.

Crispy Chicken
with Sweet and Sour Sauce (for 4)

This is one of those quickly made Chinese-style dishes which children seem to love. The golden chicken looks enticing under its coating of glossy dark sauce. Serve with plain boiled rice, and either a green salad or finely shredded white cabbage fried briefly in butter and then sprinkled with soy sauce.

4 chicken joints
2 cloves garlic, finely chopped
salt, black pepper
3 fl oz (80 ml) wine vinegar
oil for deep frying

3 tablespoons honey
1 tablespoon soy sauce
2 level teaspoons cornflour
2 tablespoons water
chopped spring onions

Put the chicken joints into a saucepan with enough hot water just to cover. Cover the pan, bring to the boil and simmer for 10 minutes. Strain off the water (you can keep this to use as stock). Add the chopped garlic, a good seasoning of salt and black pepper and the wine vinegar to the chicken in the pan. Cover again and simmer gently for another 5 minutes. Then remove the chicken joints, leaving the juices in the pan. Heat deep oil in a large frying pan and fry the chicken over a high heat until golden brown all over. Drain the joints, put into a serving dish, and keep warm while you make the sauce.

Add the honey and soy sauce to the pan juices and stir until the honey is melted. Stir the cornflour into the 2 tablespoons of water and add to the pan juices. Bring to the boil and bubble gently, stirring, for 2–3 minutes. Spoon the sauce over the chicken joints just before serving, and sprinkle on some chopped spring onions.

Grilled Chicken with Fennel Sauce (for 4)

This mild and slightly crunchy fennel sauce livens up plain grilled chicken, and it is especially good with new carrots. (It also goes well with grilled fish.)

4 joints fresh chicken
lemon juice
olive or sunflower oil
salt, black pepper

For the sauce
8 oz (225 g) fennel root
2 oz (50 g) butter

1 rounded tablespoon plain flour
1 pint (600 ml) milk
juice of ½ lemon
¼ whole nutmeg, grated
salt, black pepper
2 tablespoons hot water

Rub the chicken joints with lemon juice and oil and sprinkle with black pepper and salt. Leave at room temperature while you make the sauce. Discard any hard stalks of the fennel and chop up the rest finely. Melt the butter in a saucepan and add the fennel. Toss about over a gentle heat for 2–3 minutes. Remove from the heat and stir in the flour. Then gradually stir in the milk. Bring to the boil, stirring, then turn down the heat and simmer very gently for 10–12 minutes, stirring often. Then add the lemon juice and the grated nutmeg with salt and black pepper to taste.

Keep the sauce warm while you grill the chicken under a medium grill for 10–15 minutes on each side, according to the size of the joints. Before serving, stir 2 tablespoons hot water into the sauce. To serve, pour the sauce into a warmed serving dish and put the chicken joints on top.

Stuffed Chicken Rolls Cooked in White Wine (for 4)

These little rolls are delectable. Tender, white chicken breast fillets are wrapped round a stuffing of minced pork with rosemary and garlic, and are served under a delicate white wine and parsley sauce. It's a dish you will feel proud of, and only you will know how easy it is to make. Serve it with new potatoes when possible, or buttered noodles, and a crisp vegetable such as French beans or broccoli.

8 oz (225 g) lean minced pork	4 large chicken breast fillets
2 cloves garlic, finely chopped	1 egg, whisked
2 level teaspoons chopped rosemary	¼ pint (150 ml) dry white wine
salt, black pepper	½ teaspoon cornflour
1 tablespoon olive oil	small handful parsley, finely chopped

Mix the minced pork with the chopped garlic and rosemary and season well with salt and black pepper. Heat the olive oil in a frying pan and fry the pork in it over a fairly high heat, stirring it around with a fork to separate, for about 5 minutes. Transfer to a plate or dish and leave to cool. Skin the chicken breast fillets, cut them in half crossways and lay them spaced apart on a large sheet of greaseproof paper on a firm surface. Put another sheet of greaseproof paper on top and bash the fillets evenly with a rolling pin or other heavy implement until they are spread out and fairly thin. Sprinkle them lightly with salt.

Mix the whisked egg into the pork mixture and put a good spoonful of the stuffing on each flattened fillet. Roll the fillets carefully over the filling and place, join side down, in a fairly shallow ovenproof dish (such as an earthenware flan dish) into which the rolls will fit fairly closely. (Don't worry if bits of the stuffing fall out of the rolls either end, and sprinkle any leftover mince around the rolls.) Pour over the white wine and cover the dish with foil or a lid. Heat the oven to Gas 5/375°F/190°C. Cook the rolls in the centre of the oven for 30–35 minutes until white and just lightly cooked.

Pour all the juices off into a saucepan. In a teacup mix the cornflour with a spoonful of water until smooth and stir into the juices. Bring to the boil, stirring, and continue stirring as the sauce bubbles for 2–3 minutes. Check for seasoning, and if the sauce seems too thick stir in a little water. Finally, add the chopped parsley, spoon the sauce over the rolls, and serve.

Chicken in the Orchard Pie (for 6)

This is a rather special pie, with luxurious filling and rich, melting pastry. The sauce, made with cider, mustard and soured cream, is quite delicious. Serve the pie simply with a crisply cooked green vegetable.

For the pastry
8 oz (225 g) strong plain flour
½ teaspoon salt
4 oz (100 g) butter or margarine
2 oz (50 g) lard

For the filling
1 oz (25 g) butter or margarine
1¼–1½ lb (550–675 g) boneless chicken

1 tablespoon plain flour
½ pint (300 ml) cider
3 teaspoons fresh chopped tarragon
1 teaspoon French mustard
salt, black pepper
5 fl oz (150 ml) soured cream
1 apple, peeled, cored and thinly sliced
2 oz (50 g) mushrooms, sliced

Make the pastry first. Sift the flour and salt into a bowl, cut in the fat, and crumble with your fingertips until the mixture looks like rough breadcrumbs. Add a very little, very cold, water (the less you add the more crumbly the pastry will be). Stir in with a knife until the pastry just begins to stick together. Gather up and form into a ball, wrap in plastic or foil and put in the fridge.

Heat the oven to Gas 4/350°F/180°C. Melt the butter in a large frying pan and remove from the heat. Cut the boneless chicken into chunks and stir into the butter in the pan. Mix in the flour. Add the cider, put the pan back over the heat and stir until it bubbles and thickens. Then put in the chopped tarragon, mustard, salt and black pepper. Transfer the mixture to a casserole, cover, and cook in the oven for 1 hour.

Remove from the oven, stir in the soured cream, sliced apple and mushrooms and transfer the mixture to a suitably sized pie dish or earthenware flan dish. Allow to cool.

When the filling is cold, heat the oven to Gas 6/400°F/200°C. Knead the pastry slightly, and roll out fairly thickly into a piece big enough to cover the pie dish. Moisten the edges of the dish and lay the pastry on top. Press the edges down lightly on to the rim and trim neatly. Roll out the trimmings to decorate. Brush with a little milk, or, for a beautifully golden glaze, a little egg yolk, and cook in the centre of the oven for 25–30 minutes.

Tarragon Chicken and Mushroom Pancake Roulade (for 4–5)

The combinations of both chicken and tarragon and chicken with pancakes are well known to be delicious. In this recipe you simply make one big pancake in the oven (saving a lot of time) and then roll the creamy chicken mixture up in it like a Swiss roll. It is easy, impressive and irresistible. I don't think potatoes are necessary – just a green vegetable or green salad, and good crusty bread for the greedy!

For the pancake batter
1 oz (25 g) butter or margarine, plus some extra for greasing the roasting pan
1½ oz (40 g) plain flour
good pinch salt
1 large egg
¼ pint (150 ml) milk

For the filling
3 oz (75 g) butter

10 oz (275 g) skinned chicken breast fillets, minced or finely chopped
1 clove garlic, finely chopped
2 tablespoons plain flour
½ pint (300 ml) milk
1 good tablespoon chopped tarragon
salt, black pepper
2 oz (50 g) small mushrooms, finely sliced
grated Parmesan cheese

To make the pancake batter, melt the 1 oz (25 g) butter or margarine in a small saucepan and cool it by dipping the saucepan into a sink of cold water. Sift the flour and salt into a bowl. Make a well in the flour, break in the egg and add a little of the milk. Mix the egg and milk together with a small whisk or spatula and gradually incorporate the flour, adding more of the milk. Before you have added all the milk beat in the cooled melted butter. Add the remaining milk and whisk thoroughly until smooth and frothy. (Of course, if you have a liquidizer or food processor the batter is made in lightning time by simply whizzing up all the ingredients together.) Heat the oven to Gas 9/475°F/240°C. Then generously butter a roasting pan measuring approximately 13×9 inches (33×23 cm). Put the pan on the top shelf of the oven for a few minutes to become hot. Then pour in the batter and cook on the top shelf for 10 minutes, until risen and golden. Turn the pancake out on to a flat surface, cover with a clean damp cloth and leave to cool while you make the filling.

Melt 2 oz (50 g) of the butter in a heavy saucepan. Add the minced chicken and chopped garlic and stir and break up over the heat for 3–4 minutes; then add the flour and stir in the milk gradually. Bubble, still stirring, for 2–3 minutes, add the tarragon, and season to taste with salt and black pepper. Remove from the heat, cool a little and then add the mushrooms. Spread the mixture all over the cooled pancake and roll up from the short end like a Swiss roll. Lay the roll carefully in a shallow ovenproof dish. Smear the top of the roll with the remaining 1 oz (25 g) of soft or melted butter and sprinkle very generously with grated Parmesan. Heat the oven to Gas 4/350°F/180°C, and cook the roll on the centre shelf for 20–30 minutes.

Breast of Turkey with Cucumber and Cashews in Anchovy Sauce (for 4)

This is quickly made but extremely good. Slices of turkey breast fillet and peeled cucumber are lightly poached in stock, and then together with the crunchy cashew nuts lie under a tasty anchovy sauce topped with chopped spring onions. It's an ideal dish for weight watchers too, served simply with lightly steamed shredded cabbage sprinkled with soy sauce. But I love it with soft egg noodles!

1 lb (450 g) skinned and boned turkey
  breast
1 rather small cucumber
1 chicken stock cube
1½ pints (900 ml) water
1 clove garlic, finely chopped
1 inch (2·5 cm) piece fresh ginger,
  roughly peeled and finely chopped

2 oz (50 g) plain cashew nuts
a little butter
1 tablespoon cornflour
3 tablespoons anchovy essence
soy sauce
½ bunch spring onions

Slice the turkey fillets into thin pieces. Peel the cucumber, cut in half and then in quarters and cut into 2 inch (5 cm) strips. Dissolve the chicken cube in the water in a largish saucepan, add the chopped garlic and ginger and bring to the boil. Drop in the pieces of cucumber, return to the boil and boil for 5 minutes. Lift out the cucumber with a slotted spoon and put into a warm serving dish. Bring the stock to the boil again, add the turkey slices and boil gently for another 5 minutes. Take out the pieces, again using the slotted spoon, and add to the cucumber.

Fry the cashew nuts gently in the butter for a minute or two just until golden and add to the dish. Dissolve the cornflour in a little water and stir into the stock. Bring to the boil and bubble for about 3 minutes. Add the anchovy essence and a generous sprinkling of soy sauce. If needed, add salt and pepper to taste. Strain the sauce through a sieve on to the turkey and cucumber. (If necessary, cover the dish and keep warm in a very low oven until ready to eat.) Before serving, chop the spring onions finely, using as much of the green stalk as you can, and sprinkle on the top of the sauce.

Golden Duck with Lychee Sauce (for 4–6)

The most prized bird in China seems to call for Chinese accompaniments. Although simple to achieve, this dish is perfect for a dinner party. Both the texture and the flavour of the sauce go beautifully with the duck, which should not be overcooked – the flesh should remain slightly pink. Serve with either new potatoes or brown rice, and with sliced and steamed Chinese cabbage dotted with butter and sprinkled with a good soy sauce.

1 tablespoon caster sugar	1 level tablespoon cornflour
1 teaspoon salt	6 tablespoons water
1 small onion	2 tablespoons dry sherry
a 4¾–5 lb (2·1–2·25 kg) duck	1 bunch spring onions, finely chopped
juice of 1 orange	salt, cayenne pepper
11 oz (300 g) can lychees	

Mix the sugar and salt together and rub all over the duck. Peel and roughly chop the onion and put into the body cavity of the duck with a sprinkling of salt. Pour the orange juice also into the body cavity and then skewer up the opening to enclose. Put the duck on a rack in a roasting pan. Heat the oven to Gas 4/350°F/180°C. Put the duck in the centre of the oven for 40–45 minutes, then turn the heat up to Gas 9/475°F/240°C for another 10 minutes or so until the duck is a rich brown.

While the duck is cooking get ready to make the sauce. Strain the juices from the lychees into a small saucepan and leave on one side. Cut each lychee in half. Blend the cornflour in 2 tablespoons of the water.

When the duck is ready take out the skewers, hold the duck with a cloth and pour out the inside juices into the saucepan containing the lychee juices. Add 4 tablespoons of water and the sherry. Stir in the blended cornflour and bring to the boil, stirring until the sauce thickens. Now add the lychees and the chopped spring onions and boil again for another minute or so. Season to taste with salt and cayenne pepper. If the sauce seems too thick, stir in a little more water. Pour the sauce into a jug and pour over the carved duck on your plates.

Apricot Duck with Cashew Nuts (for 4)

Delectable in taste, festive in appearance, and not much trouble to make, this is a most useful dish. I like to serve it with brown rice and a crisp green vegetable.

4 joints of duck or 1 duck, jointed	1 large wineglass apple juice or sweet
4–5 tablespoons plain yogurt	cider
2 large cloves garlic, finely chopped	soy sauce
3 heaped teaspoons paprika	2 oz (50 g) cashew nuts
¾ teaspoon cayenne or chilli powder	chopped fresh coriander leaves,
a litle oil	parsley or mint
3 oz (75 g) dried apricots	

If the duck joints are very big, cut them in half. Mix the yogurt with the garlic, paprika and cayenne. Rub the duck pieces all over with this mixture and, if possible, leave for several hours to absorb the flavours. Then heat a very little oil in a large frying pan and fry the joints on both sides just to brown. Transfer them into a large saucepan with the dried apricots. Pour over the apple juice and about ¼ pint (150 ml) water, enough to three-quarters cover the duck. Sprinkle generously with soy sauce. Bring to the boil, then cover and simmer for ¾–1 hour until the duck is tender.

Remove the joints of duck and all the apricots and arrange on a serving dish. Keep warm in a low oven. Boil up the remaining juices fiercely until much reduced and thickened. Test for seasoning. Fry the cashew nuts in a little oil for a moment until golden. Just before serving, pour the thickened sauce over the duck and sprinkle with the nuts and coriander leaves.

Duck Divine (for 6)

This is perfect for a dinner party because it looks impressive, tastes luxurious, and is possible to prepare in advance. It is best served with brown rice and a green vegetable or salad.

a 4½–5 lb (2–2·25 kg) duck	1 glass sherry
¾–1 lb (350–450 g) piece smoked bacon flank	8 oz (225 g) black pudding, sliced
10 juniper berries, crushed	6 oz (175 g) mushrooms, sliced
2 large cloves garlic, crushed	4 oz (100 g) black olives, stoned
salt, black pepper	1 heaped tablespoon arrowroot
juice of 2 oranges	mint leaves or parsley to decorate

With a sharp knife, cut the duck in half down the breastbone. Then cut each half into three joints. Fry the joints in a little fat until golden brown all over. Put them in a large casserole with the sliced liver and heart of the duck. Cut the skin off the bacon flank and chop the bacon up into 1 inch (2·5 cm) cubes. Fry these in the pan until really crisp and brown and then add them to the duck. Add the crushed juniper berries and the garlic and season with salt and plenty of black pepper. Pour over the orange juice and sherry. Cover and cook in a pre-heated oven at Gas 4/350°F/180°C for 1–1¼ hours. Then add the black pudding and mushrooms to the casserole and cook for 20 minutes.

Remove the solid contents of the casserole with a slotted spoon and arrange them all on a large dish. Dot with the olives, cover the dish with foil and keep warm in a low oven. Drain as much fat as possible from the casserole juices. Then blend the arrowroot with a little water in a cup and add to the juices. Bring to the boil, stirring, and bubble for 2–3 minutes – the juices will thicken into a shiny sauce. Pour the sauce over the duck and the other pieces. If necessary, cover again loosely with foil and keep warm until ready to eat. Before serving, decorate all round the edge of the dish with mint leaves.

Glazed Duck with Veal and Spring Onion Rissoles (for 6–8)

This richly glossy duck cooks on the rack of the oven and its juices drip down on to the veal rissoles which are cooking below. These juices are then used to make a delectable cream sauce to go with both the duck and the rissoles. Serve with new potatoes and a crisp green vegetable such as broccoli or green beans. It should be a memorable feast!

a 4½–5 lb (2–2·25 kg) duck
1 rounded tablespoon honey
1 tablespoon soy sauce
1 lb (450 g) lean minced veal (or pie veal chopped finely in a food processor)
the duck's liver, finely chopped

1 large bunch spring onions
2 tablespoons single cream or top of the milk
2 large eggs, separated
salt, black pepper
5 fl oz (150 ml) single cream

Rub the duck with a damp cloth and then rub all over with salt. Mix the honey with the soy sauce. Smear the mixture all over the duck and leave it in a pan at room temperature for several hours if possible, basting occasionally with the liquid which has run off it. To prepare the rissoles, mix the minced veal in a bowl with the chopped duck liver. Pound with a wooden spoon until as smooth as possible. Chop the spring onions finely, using as much of the green as possible, and add to the meat. Thoroughly mix in the unbeaten egg whites and season generously with salt and black pepper. Using wet hands, take small handfuls of the meat mixture and form into short, thick sausage shapes. Lay them in a large roasting pan.

When ready to cook the duck, heat the oven to Gas 4/350°F/180°C. Pour the honey and soy juices over the rissoles in the roasting pan. Put the pan just below the centre of the oven and lay the duck simply on the centre rack just above the pan. Cook for 1½–1¾ hours (the duck becomes a very rich dark brown but if it begins to look too dark lay a piece of foil loosely on top). Make sure the juices from inside the duck pour into the roasting pan. Remove the pan and pour the excess fat off (keep it for making wonderful roast potatoes another time). Remove the rissoles with a slotted spoon and put them in a warm serving dish.

Pour the pan juices into a small saucepan, add the egg yolks and stir well, then stir in the single cream. Heat gently without allowing to boil, stirring all the time, until the sauce has thickened. Then check for seasoning and pour into a sauceboat to serve with the duck and the rissoles.

Pheasants with Cranberries and Fresh Ginger (for 8)

This is very simple to prepare, but it can make a rich and luxurious dinner party dish. Since pheasants and cranberries seem to appear on the scene at about the same time of the year it seemed natural to put them together, and everyone was pleased with the result. Serve the pheasants with new or baked potatoes and a crisp green vegetable such as broccoli or French beans. You can prepare this dish fairly well in advance, as it can be kept warm successfully in the oven.

1 oz (25 g) dried continental
  mushrooms
¼ pint (150 ml) water
2 pheasants
2 inch (5 cm) piece fresh root ginger
3 cloves garlic
2 blades mace

6 oz (175 g) fresh cranberries
3–4 strips orange peel
juice of 1 orange
salt, black pepper
1 small glass red wine
1 rounded tablespoon cornflour
handful chopped parsley to garnish

Soak the dried mushrooms in the water for at least 2 hours until soft. Then heat a little fat in the frying pan and fry the pheasants all over just to brown. Transfer to a large casserole dish. Peel the ginger and garlic and chop them together finely. Scatter the ginger and garlic over the pheasants. Add to the casserole the mace, cranberries, orange peel and juice and red wine. Strain in the water from the mushrooms, chop the mushrooms up into small pieces and add. Season well with salt and black pepper. Cover the casserole. Heat the oven to Gas 3/325°F/170°C and cook the casserole in the centre of the oven for about 2½ hours. Then remove the pheasants, carve all the flesh off and arrange it with the leg joints in a large shallow warmed serving dish. Cover with foil and put into a very low oven to keep warm.

Pour the juices from the casserole into a saucepan. Mix the cornflour with a little water until smooth, and stir into the juices. Bring to the boil, stirring, and bubble for 2 to 3 minutes. Remove from the heat, cover the saucepan and leave until ready to serve. Just before serving, reheat the sauce and pour over the pheasants. Sprinkle with chopped parsley.

Stuffed and Roasted Rabbit (for 6)

This dish is suitable for a whole, fresh rabbit. The tender delicate meat is greatly enhanced by a tasty stuffing.

1 whole fresh rabbit, 3–3½ lb (1·35–1·50kg)	the liver and kidneys of the rabbit, *or*
lemon juice	1 lamb's kidney and 4 oz (100 g)
oil	lamb's liver
salt, black pepper	4–6 oz (100–175 g) smoked bacon **finely**
For the stuffing	4 oz (100 g) mushrooms **chopped**
2 tablespoons fresh white breadcrumbs	1 large onion
	10 sage leaves
	3 cloves garlic
	1 small egg, beaten
	salt, black pepper

To make the stuffing, put the breadcrumbs in a bowl with all the chopped ingredients. Bind with the egg and season well with salt and black pepper. Mix with a wooden spoon, then press the mixture into the body cavity of the rabbit and skewer together. Rub the rabbit all over with lemon juice and oil, sprinkle with salt and black pepper, and if there is time, leave it at room temperature for an hour or more. Heat the oven to Gas 5/375°F/190°C and roast the rabbit just above the centre of the oven, basting occasionally, for 1¾–2 hours or until dark, golden brown.

Ginger Seafood in Red Pepper and Tomato Sauce with Lovage (for 8)

When trying to tell people how good this dish is I can only quote a most respected critic, Jane Grigson, who was staying with us when I made it for the first time. She said it was the best dish she had eaten for a long time, which, considering her rich gastronomic life both in England and abroad, I felt was praise indeed. Since the dish has a somewhat Indian character I serve it with basmati rice, cooked briefly and still with a bite to it. The lovage adds a distinctive flavour, but if you have none, use mint or parsley.

2 large red peppers
4 tomatoes
1 cooking apple, peeled and roughly
  chopped
juice of 1 lemon
1 lb (450 g) squid
1 lb (450 g) cod or haddock fillets
2–2½ inch (5–6·5 cm) piece fresh
  ginger

2 fresh green chillies
3–4 cloves garlic
1 large fennel root
2 oz (50 g) butter
8 oz (225 g) peeled prawns
3–4 tablespoons plain yogurt
good handful fresh lovage leaves,
  roughly chopped

Cut up the peppers roughly and boil the pieces in salted water for about 10 minutes until they are very soft. Drain. Pour boiling water over the tomatoes and then skin them. Put the peppers, the tomatoes, the peeled apple and the lemon juice into a food processor or liquidizer, and whizz until smooth. Prepare the squid by pulling out the long transparent 'backbone' and slicing the squid across in rings, discarding the goggly black eyes but keeping the tentacles, which are delicious. Cut the cod fillet into large chunks.

Peel the ginger. Cut the chillies open under running water and remove the seeds. Peel the garlic. Chop these three up together as finely as possible. Cut the fennel into largish pieces.

Heat the butter in an iron casserole, add the squid and the ginger, chilli and garlic mixture and stir around over a medium heat for a minute or two. Then add the pieces of cod and stir around for another minute. Add the fennel, pour in the pepper and tomato mixture and season with salt. Heat the oven to Gas 2/300°F/150°C. Bring the juices to the boil on top of the stove, then cover the casserole and cook in the oven for 30–40 minutes, adding the prawns for the last 5 minutes only. Keep warm in a low oven until needed. Before serving, stir in the yogurt and sprinkle with chopped lovage.

Fish Kebabs with Fennel and Cumin

(for 4)

For these kebabs I use rock salmon, which is most familiar to us when swamped in batter from the fish and chip shop. It has a somewhat meaty flavour and my daughter, eating these for the first time, thought that the fish was tender marinated lamb. Whether you find they taste like fish or meat, they are very good.

1¾ lb (800 g) rock salmon (or other firm white fish)
2 medium onions
1 large pepper
1 large fennel root

juice of 1 large lemon
6 tablespoons olive or sunflower oil
2 heaped teaspoons ground cumin
salt, black pepper

Remove the bone from the fish and cut into 1–2 inch (2·5–5 cm) pieces. Cut the onions into eighths. Cut the pepper and the fennel into pieces. Put the lemon juice and oil into a bowl and add the cumin, salt and black pepper. Add all the prepared ingredients and stir around so that they are coated with the oil mixture. Then put them on to 4–6 long skewers, alternating the ingredients but starting and ending with chunks of onion. Grill under a hot grill for 5–8 minutes on each side, basting with the remaining oil and lemon until the fish is blackened at the edges. Serve the juices as a sauce.

Fish Baked in Cabbage Leaves (for 6)

This unusual way of cooking fish in tender cabbage leaves makes it especially succulent, and the slices of sharp apples add a titillating tang.

1 lb (450 g) cod, whiting or haddock fillets
1 fairly large but loosely packed green cabbage, 1–1¼ lb (450–550 g)
1 teaspoon paprika

salt, black pepper
1 large cooking apple, about 8 oz (225 g), peeled and thinly sliced
1–2 oz (25–50 g) butter or margarine

Remove any black skin from the fish fillets. Take the whole leaves off the cabbage and submerge them in a large pan of boiling salted water for 2 minutes (you may have to do this in two or three batches). Drain and rinse with cold water. Heat the oven to Gas 5/375°F/190°C. Butter a large, but not too deep, ovenproof dish. Lay about half the cabbage leaves on the bottom, letting them come up and overlap the sides of the dish. Lay the fish fillets on top of the cabbage leaves. Sprinkle with the paprika and with salt and pepper. Arrange the apple slices on top of the fish and dot with butter. Fold the cabbage leaves over the fish and apples and cover with the remaining leaves, tucking the cabbage in round the edge so that the fish is completely encased. Dot with some more butter, cover with foil or a lid, and cook in the centre of the oven for 1 hour. Serve with boiled potatoes.

Stuffed Fish Fillets with Cream and Mushroom Sauce (for 6)

You can use any largish fish fillets for this soft, creamy dish – cod or bream are good. The stuffing is a lovely mixture of soft herring roes, tomatoes and herbs. Quick and easy to prepare, it is best with new potatoes and a crisp green vegetable.

approx. 1½ lb (675 g) filleted fish, either one large piece or several pieces
4 oz (100 g) soft herring or cod roes
2 tomatoes
1 egg
salt, black pepper

1 tablespoon chopped fresh tarragon, fennel or parsley, plus 1–2 sprigs to garnish
butter
1 small carton single cream
4 oz (100 g) mushrooms
juice of ½ lemon

Pre-heat the oven to Gas 6/400°F/200°C. Slit the fish fillets from one side with a sharp knife, not cutting right through, so as to make a pocket which you can stuff. Cut up the soft roes into small pieces and put in a mixing bowl. Pour boiling water over the tomatoes and peel them. Then chop them up small and stir into the fish roes. Lightly whisk the egg and add it together with the chopped herbs, salt and plenty of black pepper. Stuff this mixture into the fish pockets and put them in a buttered shallow ovenproof dish. Sprinkle the tops with salt and pepper and dot with butter. Cover with foil and cook in the centre of the oven for 30 minutes.

When cooked, remove from the oven and pour the butter and juices with the cream into a pan. Slice the mushrooms finely sideways, keeping the stalks on. Heat the cream and juices gently in the pan without boiling, then stir in the sliced mushrooms, together with a little salt and plenty of black pepper. Stir and let bubble for 1 minute. Take off the heat and gradually stir in the lemon juice. Pour this sauce all over the fish, decorate with a sprig or two of herbs, and serve.

Fillets of Cod with Soft Roe Sauce and Cashew Nuts (for 6–8)

Here the fish is cooked in mild coconut milk with just a hint of mace and chilli, and then served under a creamy blanket of sauce topped with golden cashew nuts. It tastes far better than I can hope to describe.

½ pint (300 ml) milk
2 oz (50 g) desiccated coconut
4 blades mace
1–2 whole dried red chillies, roughly
   broken up
2 lb (900 g) cod fillets

butter
6 oz (175 g) soft herring roes, fresh or
   tinned
salt
1 tablespoon lemon juice
2 oz (50 g) plain cashew nuts

First bring the milk to the boil in a saucepan with the coconut, the mace and the broken chillies (if you don't like too hot a flavour, remove any seeds first). Simmer gently for about 5 minutes, then cover the pan, remove from the heat and let it stand to infuse for about 30 minutes. Cut the fish into largish pieces and lay in a fairly shallow ovenproof dish. Heat the oven to Gas 6/400°F/200°C. Strain the milk through a sieve on to the fish and cover the dish with foil. Bake in the centre of the oven for 25–30 minutes, until the fish is lightly cooked. Pour the juices from the fish into a bowl. Keep the fish warm in a very low oven.

Melt a good blob of butter in a frying pan and fry the herring roes lightly for a few minutes until cooked. Sprinkle with salt. Add the roes and their buttery juice to the milky juices which the fish cooked in, and put into a liquidizer or food processor with the lemon juice. Whizz until smooth. Test for seasoning, and if the sauce has cooled re-heat it in a pan and then pour over the fish. Melt a little butter in a pan and fry the cashew nuts for about 1 minute until golden. Sprinkle them over the fish and sauce, and serve. New potatoes and baby carrots go well with this creamy dish.

Conger Eel Curry (for 4–5)

This is an aromatic rather than a hot curry, and the well-flavoured, firm flesh of the conger eel is perfect for it. It is also inexpensive, which monkfish, although an excellent alternative, is not. The fish is cooked in delicious milky juices which go perfectly with nutty rice like basmati. If you prefer potatoes to rice, cook them in the curry.

2 large cloves garlic
2 small green chillies, cut open and
  seeds removed under running
  water
1 inch (2·5 cm) piece fresh ginger,
  peeled
2 tablespoons sunflower oil
6 cardamom pods
2 lb (900 g) conger eel steaks

1 medium size red pepper, sliced in
  thin rings
3 oz (75 g) coconut flour or 3 oz
  (75 g) piece of creamed coconut
salt
½ pint (300 ml) boiling water
juice of 1 large lemon
chopped parsley to garnish, or fresh
  coriander leaves if you can get them

Chop the garlic, chillies and ginger together finely. Heat the oil in an iron casserole, and stir in the chopped ingredients and the whole cardamom pods. Add the pieces of fish and fry briefly just to seal each side. Add the sliced pepper and remove from the heat. Heat the oven to Gas 3/325°F/170°C. Put the coconut flour and 2–3 teaspoons of salt into a measuring jug, add the boiling water and stir. Pour this liquid over the fish and add the lemon juice. Bring to bubbling, cover the dish, and cook in the oven for about 45 minutes until the fish is tender. Before serving, sprinkle with chopped parsley or, preferably, fresh coriander leaves.

Smoky Fish Cakes with Tomato and Lemon Sauce (for 6)

These are a favourite for supper or Saturday lunch in our family. Even my sister, who professes to hate all fish, can't resist these crisp homemade fish cakes using smoked fish.

1 lb (450 g) potatoes
12 oz (350 g) filleted smoked
  fish
a little under ¼ pint (150 ml)
  milk
2 hard-boiled eggs, chopped
¼–½ whole nutmeg, grated
salt, black pepper
1 egg, beaten

fine semolina or ground rice to coat
  the fish cakes
oil and butter for frying

For the sauce
1 lb (450 g) squashy tomatoes
1 oz (25 g) butter
juice of 1 large lemon
1 teaspoon sugar
salt, black pepper

Peel, boil and mash the potatoes, adding a generous knob of butter. Simmer the fish in the milk in a covered saucepan for about 10 minutes or until cooked. Strain the cooking milk into the mashed potatoes and stir in. Flake the fish into the potatoes and add the chopped eggs, the nutmeg, salt and black pepper (during the summer I also add finely chopped fresh mint leaves or chives). Bind the mixture with the beaten egg. Then, using wet hands, form the mixture into ping-pong sized balls, roll in the semolina and flatten a little to make thick fish cakes. Fry in a mixture of oil and butter over a moderate heat, turning once, until rich golden brown on both sides. If necessary keep warm in a low oven.

To make the sauce, pour boiling water over the tomatoes, then skin and chop into small pieces. Put them into a saucepan with the butter, lemon juice and sugar. Cover the pan and cook gently, stirring occasionally, until you have a sauce. Season with salt and plenty of black pepper.

Sunset Pie (for 6)

So called because of its layers of yellow and orange ingredients, though of course to be completely realistic it should have red in it as well! If you really want to remedy this you could spread some tomato purée on top of the pieces of fish. Whatever you do it tastes lovely and makes a little fish go a long way.

10 oz (275 g) plain flour
½ teaspoon salt
4 oz (100 g) butter or margarine
3 oz (75 g) lard
1 large egg, beaten
1½ lb (675 g) carrots, cooked and
  chopped in small pieces

2–3 smoked cod or haddock fillets,
  about 12 oz (350 g), cut into
  chunks
4 oz (100 g) grated cheese
a few coriander seeds

Make the pastry first, as follows. Sift the flour and salt into a bowl and cut in the butter and lard. Crumble the mixture with your fingertips until it looks like rough breadcrumbs. Using a knife, mix in the beaten egg until the mixture just begins to stick together. Then press into a ball with your hands, wrap in foil or plastic, and chill in the fridge for at least 30 minutes.

Butter a 2 pint (1·1 litre) pie dish, cut off three-quarters of the pastry and knead a little to make it manageable. Roll it out and line the pie dish. Now put in the filling in layers – carrots first, then pieces of fish, then grated cheese, and so on, dotting with a few coriander seeds and seasoning with salt and pepper between each layer. End with a layer of cheese. Knead and roll out the remaining pastry into a piece big enough for the top. Moisten the edges and lay this piece over the closely filled pie, pressing down the edges a little to seal. Make 3 or 4 holes in the top with a skewer. Trim the edges and roll out the trimmings to decorate – I always cut out a fish to swim across the top of the pie! Heat the oven to Gas 4/350°F/180°C. Brush the top with a little milk and cook the pie in the centre of the oven for 1–1¼ hours. Serve with wedges of lemon and a green salad.

Fish and Mushroom Timbale (for 8)

This unusual and delicious dish, popular with both adults and children, is an impressive and inexpensive way of feeding a crowd of hungry people. It is a straightforward recipe but as it is cooked in stages, start well in advance. If you don't like fish you can use cooked chicken instead. What I particularly like is a mixture of both. Any fish of your choice will do – smoked cod is excellent, and for a special occasion the addition of prawns, mussels or salmon will turn it into a real treat.

For the rice
1 large cup (200 g) easy cook rice
2 oz (50 g) butter or margarine
1 onion, finely sliced
2 rounded teaspoons curry powder
salt

For the fish mixture
1 oz (25 g) butter or margarine

1 onion, finely sliced
4 oz (100 g) mushrooms, sliced
8 oz (225 g) fish, pre-cooked and flaked
salt, black pepper

For the crust
8 oz (225 g) packet puff pastry
a little melted butter

First soak the rice in hot water for 20–30 minutes. Then melt 2 oz (50 g) butter in a heavy-based saucepan and cook the onion gently in the butter until soft, though not brown. Stir in the curry powder and add a cup (the same one used to measure the rice) of water. Pour the soaked rice into a sieve. Rinse well under running water and add to the saucepan. Cover, bring to the boil, and simmer gently for 10–15 minutes, until the water is absorbed. Add salt to taste and leave to cool.

Meanwhile, make up the fish mixture. Melt the 1 oz (25g) butter in a frying pan and fry the onion until it is transparent. Add the mushrooms and a little more butter if necessary, and toss over the heat for just a minute or so. Mix in a bowl with the pre-cooked fish, season to taste with salt and black pepper, and leave to cool.

When the fish mixture is almost cold, butter a pudding basin or ovenproof bowl big enough to hold the rice and fish. Cut off three-quarters of the pastry and roll out very thinly, shaping it into a circle large enough to line the basin and overlap the edges, so that there will be enough to fold back over the top of the filling. Heat the oven to Gas 5/375°F190°C. Line the buttered basin with pastry and brush with some melted butter. Then roll out the last quarter of the pastry into a thin piece big enough to line the basin but not this time to overlap the edges; lay this piece over the other pastry. Then spoon in the rice and the fish mixture alternately in layers, starting and ending with a layer of rice. Fold the pastry edges over the filling to cover it, brushing with melted butter where the pastry overlaps.

Cook in the centre of the oven for 45 minutes. Turn it out on to an ovenproof serving plate and then return it to the oven for 10–15 minutes, until the dome of the pastry is golden brown all over. Serve with a simple salad.

Puddings, Cakes, Biscuits and Breads

Creamy Chocolate Truffles

These are extravagant, incredibly fattening and absolutely delicious. A treat well worth making from time to time, or a luxurious present for a greedy person.

¼ pint (150 ml) single cream
4 oz (100 g) milk chocolate ⎫
4 oz (100 g) plain chocolate ⎭ grated

1 dessertspoon strong strained tea
cocoa powder

Pour the cream into a saucepan and bring to a rolling boil. Stir in the grated chocolate and the tea and continue stirring until completely smooth. Pour on to greaseproof paper on a baking sheet. Cool and refrigerate overnight. Then leave at room temperature for an hour or so. After this, scrape up teaspoons of the mixture, dip into cocoa powder and roll into balls. Arrange separately in a box or on a tray and keep either in the fridge or in a cool place. I hope it is not necessary to say this, but eat soon!

Marquise au Chocolat (for 6)

Travelling through France one summer, we had a memorable meal at a small hotel in Brittany. The pudding was particularly luscious and the Patron scribbled a very approximate recipe on a crumpled paper napkin, giving quantities for 20 people. My family assure me that my adaptation brings back that wonderful meal to them. If you like you can make this pudding into a luxurious ice cream by putting it in the freezer.

25 sponge fingers
3 oz (75 g) granulated sugar
6 tablespoons sherry or rum
2 tablespoons water
4 oz (100 g) bitter chocolate

1 tablespoon top of the milk
½ oz (15 g) gelatine
3 eggs, separated
1 oz (25 g) caster sugar
6 fl oz (175 ml) double cream

Lay the sponge fingers in a shallow dish or tin. Dissolve the granulated sugar in the sherry and water over a low heat. Allow to bubble just for a second or two. Then spoon the hot syrup over the sponge fingers. Leave them for 30 minutes or more to absorb the syrup, turning over once.

F.F.—8

Line the bottom of a 2 pint (1·1 litre) bread tin with a piece of greaseproof paper. Line the bottom and sides of the bread tin with the sponge fingers, cutting off neatly at the top of the tin and using the bits to fill in any gaps. Melt the chocolate gently with the top of the milk. Dissolve the gelatine in a very little hot water and stir into the melted chocolate. Leave on one side to cool a little.

Whisk the egg yolks with the caster sugar until pale and thick. Whisk in the slightly cooled chocolate. Whisk the cream until thick and stir into the mixture. Whisk the egg whites until thick but not too stiff and fold gently into the chocolate and cream mixture. Spoon into the biscuit-lined tin and smooth the top. Chill thoroughly in the fridge, or in the freezer if you want it as ice cream. To turn out, slip a knife carefully round the sides and then turn out on to a serving dish. To serve, cut across in slices.

Dark Chocolate Ring (for 6–8)

What could be more tempting than a light but very chocolaty ring encasing plenty of whipped cream? During the summer fold fresh raspberries into the cream.

7 oz (200 g) caster sugar
5 large eggs, separated
2 oz (50 g) cornflour
2 oz (50 g) cocoa
pinch cream of tartar
2 oz (50 g) plain chocolate

3 tablespoons water
½ pint (300 ml) double or whipping cream
8 oz (225 g) fresh raspberries (optional)

Butter and flour an 8 inch (20 cm) ring mould tin. Heat the oven to Gas 2/300°F/150°C. Whisk the sugar and egg yolks together until pale. Sift together the cornflour and cocoa and then sift again on to the egg yolk mixture. Whisk the egg whites with the cream of tartar until stiff, and fold gently but thoroughly into the yolk mixture with the cornflour and cocoa. Pour into the prepared tin. Cook in the centre of the oven for 50–60 minutes until well risen and firm to touch. Leave in the tin for 10 minutes and then turn out on to a cooling tray.

Melt the chocolate gently with the water and stir until smooth, allow to cool slightly, and then brush all over the chocolate ring. Either sprinkle a little flaked chocolate on top, or decorate with fresh raspberries if you are using them in the cream. When cold, transfer the ring to a serving plate and fill with whipped cream and fresh raspberries if available.

Austrian Chocolate Ring with Raspberry Sauce (for 8)

No flour goes into this rich, moist pudding cake, only almonds and a few breadcrumbs. It is iced with glossy chocolate and served with a lovely fresh raspberry sauce.

4 oz (100 g) butter
4 oz (100 g) icing sugar
5 eggs, separated
2 oz (50 g) almonds in their skins,
  ground finely in a liquidizer
1½ oz (40 g) fresh white breadcrumbs
½ oz (15 g) finely ground coffee
2 oz (50 g) plain chocolate
1 tablespoon water
pinch salt

For the icing
3 oz (75 g) plain chocolate
2 tablespoons water
2 tablespoons rum or brandy

For the sauce
4 oz (100 g) caster sugar
juice of 1 lemon
4 tablespoons water
8 oz (225 g) fresh or frozen
  raspberries

Butter and flour a 9–10 inch (23–25 cm) ring mould tin. Beat the butter until soft. Add the icing sugar and beat until light and fluffy. Add the egg yolks one at a time, beating in between. Then beat in the ground almonds, the breadcrumbs and coffee. Melt the chocolate in the water and beat thoroughly into the mixture. Heat the oven to Gas 3/325°F/170°C. Whisk the egg whites with a pinch of salt until thick but not stiff, and fold carefully into the yolk and chocolate mixture with a metal spoon. Pour into the prepared tin. Bake in the centre of the oven for about 45 minutes, until a knife slipped in the centre comes out clean. Leave in the tin to cool, then loosen the edges carefully and turn out.

To make the icing, gently melt the chocolate with the water and rum and stir until smooth. Cool slightly and then spread all over the chocolate ring. If liked, shave a few sprinklings of fine chocolate on to the top.

To make the sauce, dissolve the caster sugar in the lemon juice and water over a gentle heat. Stir in the raspberries and remove from the heat after about ½ minute. Then put the mixture into a liquidizer and whizz until smooth. Pour the sauce into a serving jug and leave to cool. You can serve the ring just with the raspberry sauce if you like, but I think a slice of the cake covered with a mingling of raspberry sauce and cream is sheer heaven.

Iced Lemon Soufflé in a Chocolate Case

(for 8)

This was an experiment which I am particularly pleased with and repeat often for dinner parties because it always provokes gasps of wonder. The thin and jagged casing of dark chocolate, looking like the bark of some exotic tree, encases a pale and light lemon soufflé. The combination of flavour and texture could hardly be more mouth-watering.

6 oz (175 g) plain chocolate, plus
  extra for decoration
3 tablespoons water
½ oz (15 g) butter
grated rind and juice of 2 large
  lemons

6 oz (175 g) caster sugar
4 large eggs, separated
½ oz (15 g) gelatine
½ pint (300 ml) double cream

Oil a 7½–8 inch (19–20 cm) loose-based cake tin well, and line the base with a disc of oiled greaseproof paper. Break up the chocolate and melt with 1 tablespoon of the water in a double saucepan or in a bowl set over a pan of hot water. When melted, stir in the butter. Spoon the chocolate on to the base of the cake tin and spread evenly with a spatula all over the bottom and up the sides of the tin, leaving a rough and uneven edge. Leave to become firm while you make the soufflé.

Add the finely grated lemon rind and the caster sugar to the egg yolks and whisk until the mixture is pale and thick. Squeeze the lemon juice into a saucepan and add the remaining 2 tablespoons of water. Sprinkle in the gelatine and dissolve in the liquid over a gentle heat, but don't let it boil. Pour the hot liquid slowly on to the egg yolk mixture, whisking all the time. Continue to whisk until cooled a bit and just beginning to thicken. Whisk the cream until thick but not stiff, and fold into the lemon mixture. Then whisk the egg whites until they stand in soft peaks and fold in with a metal spoon. Pour into the chocolate-lined tin – the edge of the chocolate should be a little above the top of the soufflé. Freeze for at least 2 hours.

To unmould, rub the sides of the frozen tin with a hot cloth and then, using a small and very sharp knife, cut down between the chocolate sides and the tin until it is loosened enough all round to push up. (I find the easiest way is to put the tin on top of a jam jar and then push down.) Separate the chocolate base from the base of the tin with a knife if necessary, and then carefully peel off the greaseproof paper. Put on a serving dish and re-freeze until about 1 hour before you eat; then decorate the soufflé top with chocolate shavings and move the soufflé to the main part of the fridge, as it is most delicious eaten very cold, but not quite frozen.

Snowballs (for 6)

Children love watching these being made, and everyone appreciates their melting consistency and flavour. During the summer you can put strawberries or raspberries among the snowballs, which makes them even more irresistible.

6 egg whites	1 pint (600 ml) milk
pinch salt	2 level tablespoons caster sugar
2 rounded tablespoons icing sugar, sifted	1 teaspoon vanilla essence
6 egg yolks	a few chopped nuts

Whisk the egg whites with a pinch of salt until thick, and then beat in the sifted icing sugar. Bring a saucepan of water to a fierce boil and drop in teaspoons of the egg whites, one or two at a time, turning them over in the water once and taking them out with a slotted spoon as they puff up. Don't leave them in the water for more than a moment as they will tend to go soggy. Pile them in a serving bowl.

Put the egg yolks in the top of a double saucepan and beat lightly together. Stir in the milk, the caster sugar and the vanilla essence. Stir over very gently simmering water until thickened to the consistency of thin cream. Leave to become completely cold, then stir round and pour over the snowballs, first draining off any water that may have accumulated in the bowl. Sprinkle with a few chopped nuts and serve.

Cream of Yogurt Dessert (for 4)

This is simply homemade yogurt made with cream instead of milk, and it is a delicious base for all sorts of fruit toppings, purées or sauces as it sets more firmly than normal yogurts. (You can of course make ordinary yogurt with milk by this same method.)

1 pint (600 ml) single cream, or
  double if you are feeling lavish
1 tablespoon commercial plain yogurt

Bring the cream to the boil in a saucepan, then lower the heat immediately and let it hardly simmer for 2–3 minutes. Remove from the heat, put a food thermometer in the pan and leave until it has gone down to 125°F/50°C (usually the yogurt-making temperature is marked). If you have no thermometer, the correct temperature is reached when you can just bear to dip your finger in the cream and keep it there for 10 seconds, though I never think this method is so reliable as people have such different levels of tolerance to heat. If you allow the cream to become too cold by mistake you can always heat it a little and get it to the right temperature again.

Meanwhile put 4 individual bowls or one larger bowl if you prefer in a warm place or airing cupboard. When the cream has reached the right temperature, stir the commercial yogurt in a warm bowl with a little of the cream until smooth. Then stir in the rest of the cream a little at a time until well mixed. Pour the mixture in to the serving dishes and cover with foil or plastic film, and then cover with a small folded blanket to keep the yogurt at the same temperature. Leave for 6–8 hours until it is thickly set. (Never leave the yogurt in the warm for longer than is necessary to set it, as it will become more sour and it is the mild creamy flavour, so different to sharp commercial yogurt, which makes it so worthwhile.) Refrigerate well.

You can eat the yogurt either plain or sprinkled with brown sugar. I stir whatever soft fruit is available with some lemon juice into either sugar syrup or honey, and spoon the mixture on top of the yogurt before serving. Alternatively you can used stewed fruit in thick syrup, or in mid-winter stewed dried apricots are mouth-watering.

Antonia's Cheesecake (for 8)

This rich and creamy cheesecake is a great favourite. It is good just on its own, but particularly mouth-watering served with a sharp fruit purée such as blackcurrant or damson, or in the winter with rhubarb.

7 oz (200 g) digestive biscuits
3 oz (75 g) butter
1 oz (25 g) brown sugar
12 oz (350 g) cream cheese
1 level tablespoon cornflour
2 tablespoons cream or top of the
 milk

1 oz (25 g) melted butter
1 heaped tablespoon caster sugar,
 preferably kept in a jar with vanilla
 pods
pinch salt
2 egg whites

Crumble the digestive biscuits either in a liquidizer or under a rolling pin. Melt the 3 oz (75 g) butter with the brown sugar and mix thoroughly into the biscuit crumbs. Press the mixture evenly with a metal spoon over the base and sides of a 10 inch (25 cm) flan dish. Refrigerate while you prepare the filling.

Soften the cream cheese in a bowl with an electric whisk or a wooden spoon. Mix the cornflour to a smooth paste with the cream or milk and add to the cream cheese together with the melted butter and caster sugar. Mix thoroughly. Heat the oven to Gas 3/325°F/170°C. Add the salt to the egg whites, whisk until thick but not stiff, and fold gently into the cream cheese mixture with a metal spoon. Pour into the biscuit crust and bake in the centre of the oven for 30–40 minutes until lightly set. Allow to cool.

Banana and Mint Meringue Ice Cream Cake (for 10)

This is ideal for a large family lunch or for a party. It is very convenient as it can be made the day before or even earlier if you like. The layers of rich banana with a lemony tang alternating with crisp mint meringue seem irresistible to most people.

7 oz (200 g) icing sugar

3 large eggs

2–3 drops peppermint essence

8 oz (225 g) bananas

juice of ½ lemon

pinch salt

6 oz (175 g) demerara sugar

6 tablespoons water

½ pint (300 ml) double cream

shavings or grated plain chocolate to
  decorate

Sift the icing sugar into a bowl. Separate the eggs, putting them into two large bowls. Set the yolks aside for the ice cream. Whisk the egg whites until they stand in soft peaks, then whisk in the sifted icing sugar a little at a time. Add the peppermint essence. Put the bowl over a large pan half filled with gently simmering water and continue whisking for about 5 minutes until very stiff. Heat the oven to Gas 2/300°F/150°C. Put a large sheet of greaseproof paper on a baking sheet and spread the meringue mixture over it about 1 inch (2·5 cm) thick. Put the baking sheet on the bottom shelf of the oven and cook for 1¼–1¾ hours until the meringue is firm and dry.

Now start to make the ice cream. Purée the bananas with the lemon juice until smooth. Whisk the egg yolks, with the salt added, until pale and thickly creamy. Dissolve the demerara sugar in the water in a pouring saucepan over a low heat. Then boil fiercely for 3 minutes and pour immediately in a thin stream on to the egg yolks, whisking all the time at high speed. Continue whisking for at least 5 minutes until pale and thick. Then whisk in the banana purée. In another large bowl whisk the cream until thick but not stiff. Pour the banana and egg yolk mixture into the cream and fold in thoroughly with a large metal spoon.

Now turn the cooked meringue upside down, peel off the greaseproof paper, and then break up the meringue only roughly. In a deep 8 inch (20 cm) cake tin make layers of the ice cream mixture and the meringue, starting and ending with a layer of ice cream. Freeze. When well frozen turn the ice cream cake on to a serving plate by rubbing the outside of the tin with a hot cloth until it slips out. Sprinkle shavings of plain chocolate on the top and refreeze until ready to eat.

Fresh Orange Ice Cream Cake (for 8–10)

A sumptuous party ice cream made with fresh oranges, eggs and cream. The eggs are separated so that the cake has stripes of tangy orange and a white meringue mixture into which are incorporated crumbled sponge fingers. Beautiful and irresistible.

3 medium to large oranges	6 tablespoons water
12 oz (350 g) granulated sugar	juice of 1 lemon
2 large eggs, separated	1 packet sponge fingers
½ pint (300 ml) whipping cream	

Grate the rind of 2 of the oranges. Then squeeze out the juice and pour into a measuring jug – it should be about ¼ pint (150 ml), but if it is not make it up with more orange or lemon juice. Put the orange rind and juice and 6 oz (175 g) of the sugar into a pouring saucepan. Put the egg yolks into the mixing bowl of an electric whisk. Put the pan of orange juice and sugar over a low heat and stir until the sugar is dissolved. Then increase the heat and boil fiercely without stirring for 3 minutes. Pour immediately on to the egg yolks in a thin stream, whisking all the time at high speed. Continue whisking until thick and pale orange. In another bowl whisk the cream until thick and then whisk in the orange and egg yolk mixture. Put in the fridge while you prepare the white meringue ice cream.

Whisk the egg whites in a bowl with an electric whisk until they stand in soft peaks. Then put the remaining 6 oz (175 g) of sugar in a pouring saucepan with the water. As before, stir to dissolve the sugar over a low heat and then boil fiercely without stirring for 3 minutes. Pour the syrup in a thin stream on to the whisked egg whites, whisking all the time at high speed. Continue whisking until thick and white. Gradually whisk in the lemon juice. Crush the sponge fingers roughly under a rolling pin and stir into the egg white mixture.

To assemble the cake, peel the remaining orange and cut into the thinnest possible segments, using a sharp knife and removing any pips and as much pith as possible. Arrange in a circular pattern on the bottom of a deep 7½–8 inch (18·5–20 cm) diameter cake tin. Then spoon in half the orange mixture, then all of the white meringue mixture and finally the remaining orange mixture. Freeze thoroughly, overnight if possible. To turn the cake out, rub the tin all over with a cloth dipped in very hot water until it will slip out of the tin on to a serving plate or cake stand. (If it is a loose-based tin, just rub the sides, then press the cake out, rub the remaining base and carefully remove.) Put the cake back in the freezer until ready to serve.

Brandy Crunch Iced Parfait (for 8–10)

Everyone votes this one of the best ice creams. Rich but light, it has a contrasting crunch of toasted biscuits. Armagnac brandy is specially good if you have it. It gives a sophisticated flavour but all the children I have tried it on have consumed it with gusto. (For a special occasion, mix a heaped tablespoon of caster sugar with 2 oz (50 g) flaked almonds and toss around in a dry, hot pan until they have caramelized. Stir the nuts as they cool on a plate to keep them separate, and then top the ice cream with them when it has frozen.)

1 packet plain digestive biscuits	3 egg yolks
2 tablespoons caster sugar	1 teaspoon vanilla essence
3 egg whites	½ pint (300 ml) single cream
pinch salt	½ pint (300 ml) double cream
8 oz (225 g) granulated sugar	2–3 tablespoons brandy
¼ pint (150 ml) water	

Crush the biscuits under a rolling pin and then mix in a bowl with the caster sugar. Heat a large frying pan until very hot and then stir the crushed biscuits around in it for a minute or two until crisp and toasted. In an electric whisk if possible, whisk the egg whites with the salt until they form soft peaks. Dissolve the granulated sugar in the water in a pan over a gentle heat. Then increase the heat and boil fiercely without stirring for 3 minutes. Pour immediately on to the egg whites in a thin stream, whisking fast all the time. Continue whisking until you have a thick, white meringue mixture. Then whisk in the egg yolks and the vanilla essence. Put the creams together in a bowl and whisk until thick but not stiff. Fold the cream into the egg mixture and gradually stir in the brandy to taste. Lastly, gently fold in the toasted biscuits, pour the mixture into a serving bowl, and freeze for several hours.

This ice cream does not need stirring half-way through the freezing. I often make it a day or two in advance and you will find it is soft enough to eat even straight from the freezer, but the best thing is to move it into the freezer compartment of the fridge an hour or two before serving.

Passionate Parfait (for 8–10)

Here is a real treat – passion fruit ice cream. The taste and texture is so exquisite that even this generous quantity won't last very long. Serve it with some sharp lemon biscuits – you could use the egg yolks left over from the ice cream to make them.

3 large egg whites	4 fresh passion fruit
pinch salt	juice of 1 large lemon
8 oz (225 g) granulated sugar	½ pint (300 ml) double or whipping
¼ pint (140 ml) water	cream

Whisk the egg whites and salt until they stand in soft peaks. Dissolve the sugar in the water in a saucepan over a low heat, then boil fiercely for 3 minutes. Pour immediately in a thin stream on to the egg whites, whisking all the time at high speed. Continue whisking until it looks like a thick white meringue mixture. Cut the passion fruit in half and scoop out the insides with a teaspoon, including the pips. Whisk into the meringue mixture, adding the lemon juice. Whisk the cream in a separate bowl until thick but not stiff, and then fold gently but thoroughly into the meringue mixture. Transfer to a serving bowl and freeze for at least 3 hours.

Elderflower and Gooseberry Ice Cream

(for 8)

In early summer the drab-looking elder bursts into blossom all around us, and at the same time the first cooking gooseberries arrive in the shops and markets. The marriage of the two, as country people have known for years, is exquisite. My children pick me elderflowers as they walk across the common on the way home from school, and for weeks my fridge is full of delicate elderflower cordial and elderflower and gooseberry or apricot fool, while in my freezer are ice creams and sorbets all with the subtle scent and flavour of Muscatel grapes which the modest elderflower so magically imparts. The following is a very simple method of making ice cream which you can use with any good fruit mush or purée.

10–15 elderflower heads
1 lb (450 g) gooseberries, topped and
   tailed

5 oz (150 g) sugar
1 tablespoon lemon juice
½ pint (300 ml) double cream

Shake and lightly pull the flowers off the elder stems and put in a saucepan. Add the gooseberries, the sugar and enough water almost to cover. Bring to the boil, then cover and simmer, stirring once or twice, until the mixture is completely mushy. Add the lemon juice and let it become completely cold. Then whisk up the cream until thick but not stiff and mix gently into the gooseberry mixture. Put into a dish and freeze. About half an hour before serving, take the dish out of the freezer and leave in the fridge to ripen and soften slightly.

Apricot Ice Cream
with Toasted Almonds (for 6–8)

In my experience a good home-made ice cream causes more pleasure and enjoyment than any other pudding you could serve. Try this offering, which combines creamy richness with the strong flavour of dried apricots enhanced by a toasted crunch of almonds.

8 oz (225 g) dried apricots
8 oz (225 g) light brown sugar
¼ pint (150 ml) water
juice of 1 lemon
3 large eggs, separated
½ pint (300 ml) double cream

2 oz (50 g) flaked almonds, toasted
   for a few minutes in a hot oven until
   brown
salt
3 oz (75 g) icing sugar, sifted

Soak the apricots in water for 2 hours or more until soft. Drain and chop into small pieces. Dissolve the brown sugar in the water over a low heat. Add the chopped apricots. Bring to bubbling and stir. Cover the pan, lower the heat, and allow to simmer very gently for 10–15 minutes, stirring now and then. Remove from the heat and stir in the lemon juice. Whisk the egg yolks and stir them into the apricots. Put the pan back over a very low heat, stirring constantly without allowing to bubble for 5 minutes. Transfer the mixture to a bowl and leave to cool.

Whisk the cream until thick but not stiff and fold it into the apricot mixture. Stir in all but a handful of the flaked almonds. Whisk the egg whites with a good pinch of salt until thick. Then add the icing sugar and whisk until the mixture stands in peaks. Fold in the apricot and cream mixture with a metal spoon. Pour into a pretty bowl and sprinkle the remaining almonds on top. Freeze for several hours.

Apricot Mountain (for 6–8)

Layers of apricots and sultanas with cream and rum make a delicious winter pudding to cheer the greyest day. I always think dried apricots have a better flavour than fresh ones because it is so intense; I often use them during the summer as well as in winter.

8 oz (225 g) dried apricots	juice of 1 lemon
12 oz (350 g) sultanas	3 tablespoons rum
2 oz (50 g) candied peel	½ pint (300 ml) double or whipping
8 tablespoons soft pale brown sugar	cream

Put the apricots into one bowl and the sultanas into another. Soak both in water for at least 2 hours. Then drain the fruit and put into separate saucepans. Add the candied peel, 4 oz (100 g) of the sugar and the juice of half the lemon to the sultanas and add enough water almost to cover. Add the remaining sugar and lemon juice to the apricots and add water to cover. Put lids on the saucepans, bring to the boil, and simmer for ¾–1 hour until the fruits have gone fairly thick and mushy – you may have to boil up the sultana mixture fiercely at the end to thicken the syrup. Remove from the heat and stir 1 tablespoon of the rum into the sultanas and 2 tablespoons into the apricots. Leave the fruits to become completely cold.

Whisk the cream until thick. Spoon the fruits and cream into a glass dish in thin layers. Start with apricots, then sultanas, then cream and so on, ending with a sprinkling of sultanas. The mixture should be thick enough to build up to a luscious layered mountain within the glass dish. Chill in the fridge until ready to eat.

Almond Dreams with Lychees (for 6)

Extremely refreshing after a rich meal, this is an easy to make and
rather magical Chinese dessert. Almond Dreams are translucent white
softly jellied squares with a delicate flavour of almond. They look
strange and beautiful in a bowl topped with scented lychees under a
glossy syrup. (If you hate the flavour of almond, omit the essence and
add 1 tablespoon of strong rosewater to the liquid before cooling.) In
summer make these jellied squares as an accompaniment to soft fruit.

2 × ½ oz (2 × 15 g) packets gelatine	¼ teaspoonful almond essence
4 tablespoons + 1 pint (600 ml) hot water	2 × 11 oz (2 × 300 g) cans lychees
¾ pint (450 ml) milk	1 tablespoon lemon juice
3 tablespoons sugar	4 oz (100 g) caster sugar

Lightly oil a cake tin or roasting tin about 9×9 inches (23×23 cm). Put
the gelatine into a bowl with the 4 tablespoons of water and put the
bowl over a saucepan of very hot water. Stir until dissolved. In another
saucepan heat 1 pint (600 ml) water with the milk, the 3 tablespoons of
sugar and the almond essence. Stir until the sugar is dissolved, and then
stir in the dissolved gelatine. Pour into the cake tin and leave to cool.
Then chill in the fridge until set.

Meanwhile drain the juices from the cans of lychees into a saucepan
and add the lemon juice and caster sugar. Put over the heat, stir until
the sugar has dissolved, then bring to the boil and boil fiercely without
stirring for 5 minutes. When the almond mixture is set, loosen the edges
with a sharp knife and cut into 1 inch (2·5 cm) squares. Turn out
carefully into a pretty glass bowl, arranging some of the squares up the
sides of the bowl to make a depression in the middle. Shortly before
serving, spoon the lychees into the middle and spoon the syrup over
them. Keep in the fridge until ready to serve.

Strawberry and Pineapple Salad with Orange Cream (for 6–8)

This is simply a magical blend of fruit with a luscious cream to go with it.

1 lb (450 g) fresh strawberries
1 small pineapple
2–3 tablespoons caster sugar
juice of 1 lemon

½ pint (300 ml) double cream
grated rind and juice of 1 small
 orange

Cut the strawberries in half only if they are very large. Cut the skin off the pineapple and cut into smallish pieces. Mix with the strawberries in a glass bowl. Gently mix in the sugar and the lemon juice. Whisk the cream until thick but not too stiff, and then gradually stir in the orange juice and the grated rind. Serve the cream in a separate bowl to spoon over the fruit salad on your plate.

Winter Raspberries (for 8)

This mousse, a luxurious echo of summer, is so easy to make that it almost feels like cheating. It can be made well ahead for a dinner party. Serve it with light, thin biscuits.

1 packet raspberry or strawberry jelly
½ pint (300 ml) boiling water
2 tablespoons caster sugar
5 fl oz (150 ml) carton soured cream
½ pint (300 ml) double or whipping
 cream

1 tablespoon lemon juice
1 lb (450 g) frozen, unsweetened
 raspberries
chopped nuts or flaked chocolate to
 decorate

Break up the jelly into a bowl. Pour over the boiling water and stir until dissolved. Stir in the caster sugar, add the soured cream and whisk until smooth. Whisk the double cream until thick but not stiff, and then whisk gently into the jelly mixture. Whisk in the lemon juice, a little at a time. Empty in the frozen raspberries straight from the freezer and separate with a fork until there is no piece bigger than a single fruit left. (Stirring the raspberries in while they are still frozen helps to set the mixture as you do it and so prevents the fruit from sinking to the bottom of the cream.)

Pour the mixture into a pretty serving bowl or individual glasses and put at once in the bottom of the fridge for 2–3 hours, or longer if possible. Decorate the top of the mousse with chopped nuts or flaked chocolate.

Lovely Lemon Ring (for 5–6)

I have a particular passion for any sweet made with lemons, and this delicately textured ring is truly exquisite. It has a delicious shiny lemon curd top and creamy honeycombed base, and it slips down the throat in the most irresistible way.

1 oz (25 g) self-raising flour, sifted
8 oz (225 g) caster sugar
pinch salt
finely grated rind of 1 lemon
3 tablespoons lemon juice (approx. 1 lemon)

3 large eggs, separated
½ pint (300 ml) single cream
chopped toasted nuts to garnish (optional)

Mix together the sifted flour, the caster sugar and the salt. Sift into a mixing bowl and stir in the lemon rind and juice. In another bowl whisk the egg yolks with an electric whisk until pale and creamy. Stir into the flour, sugar and lemon mixture. Then stir in the single cream gradually. Put a roasting pan full of warm water on the centre shelf of the oven and heat the oven to Gas 3/325°F/170°C. Then whisk the egg whites until they hold soft peaks and fold them gently into the yolk and lemon mixture using a large metal spoon. Pour into a wetted 2 pint (1·1 litre) ring mould tin and set it in the pan of water in the oven. Cook for 1 hour. Allow to cool (it will sink a bit as it cools), and when very cold loosen the edges carefully and turn out, giving a shake, on to a serving plate. If liked, sprinkle the top with chopped toasted nuts. Refrigerate until needed.

Apricot and Guava Tart (for 8)

This is one of our favourite Sunday lunch puddings, especially in winter when the variety of fruit is limited and we are tired of apple pies. Serve hot or warm with plenty of cream.

For the pastry
8 oz (225 g) plain flour
4 oz (100 g) butter } cold from
2 oz (50 g) vegetable fat } the fridge
1 egg
1 egg yolk

For the filling
8 oz (225 g) dried apricots, soaked in
  water for several hours or overnight
14 oz (400 g) can guavas
rind and juice of 1 lemon
4 oz (100 g) pale brown or demerara
  sugar
1 packet sponge fingers
2 oz (50 g) caster sugar
1 egg white

Remember to soak the apricots for the filling, and then make the pastry. Sift the flour into a bowl. Cut the butter and fat into small pieces and then crumble them into the flour with your fingertips until the mixture looks like breadcrumbs. Whisk the egg and egg yolk (keep the white for glazing the pastry at the end) together and then, using a knife, stir them into the flour mixture until it begins to stick together. Then gather it up into a ball, wrap in cling film, and leave in the fridge for at least 30 minutes.

When the apricots are soaked, drain them and put them in a saucepan with the strained juice from the can of guavas. Coarsely grate the lemon rind and leave on one side. Squeeze the juice and add it to the apricots. Add the brown sugar. Bring the apricots to the boil, stirring until the sugar is dissolved, then cover and simmer gently for 20–30 minutes until the apricots are soft. Then uncover the saucepan and boil over a high heat for 3–5 minutes until they are syrupy and somewhat thickened. Break up the sponge fingers roughly and spread over the bottom of a 9 inch (23 cm) earthenware flan dish. Spoon the apricots and juices over the sponge fingers. Cut the guava halves into 2–3 slices each and arrange them evenly on top of the apricots. Finally, scatter over the grated lemon rind. Put the dish in a cool place to become cold.

Roll out the pastry on a floured surface in a circle slightly larger than the flan dish. Moisten the edges of the dish and place the pastry on top. Cut round the edge neatly, gather up the scraps of pastry and roll out to cut out decorations. Thoroughly mix the caster sugar with the egg white with a small whisk or fork, and brush this glaze all over the pastry.

Heat the oven to Gas 6/400°F/200°C and cook the tart in the centre of the oven for 30–40 minutes until the glazed crust is an uneven dark brown. (You can either keep this tart in a low oven until needed, or re-heat it.)

Ace Apricot Tart (for 7–8)

It is surprising that something so easy to do can be as special as this rich tart made with dried apricots. It is cooked upside down, which makes the biscuit crust pastry extra crisp, while the apricots have a wonderfully intense flavour cooked in a goo of butter and sugar. The tart is more than perfect served warm with whipped cream, but is also excellent cold if there is any left over, which in our family hardly ever happens.

For the pastry
6 oz (175 g) plain flour
pinch salt
3 oz (75 g) caster sugar
3 oz (75 g) butter
1 egg, whisked

For the filling
8 oz (225 g) dried apricots
2 oz (50 g) butter
6 oz (175 g) caster sugar

First leave the apricots to soak in a bowl of water for 2 hours or more, overnight if you like. Meanwhile, make the pastry. Sift the flour and salt into a bowl. Stir in the sugar. Just melt the butter gently and mix into the flour with a wooden spoon. Then thoroughly mix in the whisked egg until the dough is smooth. Press the mixture together, cover with cling film and leave in the fridge for at least 1 hour.

Smear the bottom and sides of a 9 inch (23 cm) flan dish or tin (not one with a loose base) with the 2 oz (50 g) filling butter. Sprinkle the 6 oz (175 g) caster sugar all over the bottom of the flan dish on top of the butter. Then drain the apricots and pat dry with absorbent paper. Arrange the apricots neatly in circles on top of the sugar. Now take the pastry from the fridge and press into a ball. Roll out on a floured surface to the size of the flan dish. Roll the pastry back over the rolling pin gently as it breaks easily, and then out again on to the flan dish. (If the pastry does break, just press it together again – don't worry if it looks messy, as it won't show.) Press the edges of the pastry firmly down within the flan dish. Pierce two or three holes in the pastry. Heat the oven to Gas 6/400°F/200°C, and cook the tart in the centre of the oven for 25 minutes. Then turn down the oven to Gas 3/325°F/170°C and cook for a further 30–35 minutes. Remove from the oven, cool slightly, then turn out on to a serving plate and eat while still warm, with cream if you like.

Tarte de Fruits Divers (for 8–10)

I find this the most successful and scrumptious fruit tart. It is made with a mixture of dried fruit and cooked upside down like the French 'Tarte Tatin' with a crunchy pastry. It looks most impressive, and is best served lukewarm, with cream only for real guzzlers as it is wonderfully rich with a buttery caramelized flavour.

For the pastry
6 oz (175 g) plain flour
2 oz (50 g) fine semolina
2 oz (50 g) caster sugar
4 oz (100 g) soft butter
1 large egg, lightly whisked

For the fruit mixture
4 oz (100 g) dried apricots
4 oz (100 g) dried peaches
4 oz (100 g) dried pears
4 oz (100 g) prunes
3–4 oz (75–100 g) unsalted butter
4 oz (100 g) caster sugar

Put the apricots, peaches and pears to soak in a bowl of water for several hours, or overnight if you like. Meanwhile make the pastry. Sift the flour into a bowl and stir in the semolina and caster sugar. Work in the soft butter with a wooden spoon and then work in the whisked egg to form a dough. Gather into a ball, wrap in cling film and refrigerate.

When the soaking fruit is well plumped, pour boiling water on to the prunes and leave for a little while until you can extract the stones easily. Drain all the fruit. Dot or smear the bottom of a 10–11 inch (25–28 cm) fluted earthenware flan dish with the unsalted butter, and spread the caster sugar evenly on top. Arrange the fruit face downwards in as artistic a pattern as you can. Now take the pastry from the fridge, knead it slightly, and roll it out on a well-floured board into a circle just big enough to cover the flan dish. Roll the pastry back over the rolling pin and put it on top of the fruit. (If the pastry should break, don't worry, just press it together over the top; as it turns out underneath the tart it won't matter.) Press the edges of the pastry well down into the flan dish. (If there is time, refrigerate the tart for a little before cooking.)

Heat the oven to Gas 7/425°F/220°C and cook the tart towards the top of the oven for 30–40 minutes, or until the pastry is very dark brown. Then lower the oven heat to Gas 2/300°F/150°C and cook for a further ½–¾ hour. Turn off the heat and leave the tart in the oven for 10 minutes or more before turning out carefully on to a large circular serving plate.

Boiled Fruit Cake

This cake is so simple to make that I find it invaluable during the school holidays and for school bazaars and fêtes. It also makes a most welcome present. The old-fashioned method (I learnt about it in Ireland) of first boiling the fruit with the sugar, butter and water plumps the fruit up and gives a lovely fudgy flavour to the cake. It's the easiest way to make an excellent fruit cake which stays fresh and moist for a long time. You can alter the combination of the fruit as you like, and it makes it extra delicious to add 2–3 oz (50–75 g) walnut pieces with the fruit. If you like, you can also use wholemeal flour, which adds a nutty flavour.

6 oz (175 g) butter or margarine
6 oz (175 g) soft brown sugar
½ pint (300 ml) water
4 oz (100 g) raisins
4 oz (100 g) sultanas
4 oz (100 g) currants

2 oz (50 g) candied peel
8 oz (225 g) plain flour
1 teaspoon bicarbonate of soda
½–1 teaspoon freshly ground nutmeg
2 large eggs, beaten

Dissolve the butter and sugar in the water in a saucepan. Add the fruit, bring to the boil, cover the pan and simmer gently for 10 minutes. Allow to cool. Sift the flour and bicarbonate of soda into a mixing bowl and add the nutmeg. Add the fruit mixture and stir with a wooden spoon. Add the beaten eggs and mix thoroughly. Heat the oven to Gas 4/350°F/180°C. Put a disc of greased paper on the bottom of a greased deep 6–7 inch (15–17·5 cm) cake tin and pour in the cake mixture. Bake in the centre of the oven for 1–1¼ hours. Leave in the tin for 10 minutes, then loosen the sides with a knife and turn out carefully on to a rack to cool.

VARIATION
Prune, Walnut and Orange Cake. Make this in the same way as the boiled fruit cake, but use white sugar instead of brown and for the fruit combination use 6 oz (175 g) pitted prunes, chopped up roughly, 4 oz (100 g) raisins, 2 oz (50 g) sultanas, 2 oz (50 g) walnut pieces and the coarsely grated rind of 1 large orange with the juice replacing part of the boiling water. Add no spice.

The Ultimate Chocolate Cake (for 10-12)

I love real chocolate cake (no relation to dry and tasteless chocolate sponge) and am always experimenting with different mixtures. To me this is the best of them all. The divine flavour of hazelnuts and dark chocolate, with a hint of bitter orange combined with such a delicate, moist texture – rather like very light fudge – always provokes the most ecstatic appreciation. The cake may be extravagant with ingredients, but to me it is worth every penny. It is a crumbling cake which should be eaten with a fork, so it makes a perfect pudding, with cream if you like.

8 oz (225 g) plain dark chocolate
8 oz (225 g) butter
6 oz (175 g) caster sugar
6 eggs
8 oz (225 g) ground hazelnuts (these can be ground in either a food processor or a coffee grinder)
4 oz (100 g) fresh breadcrumbs, brown or white

finely grated rind of 2 oranges
a little orange marmalade

For the chocolate glaze
4 oz (100 g) plain dark chocolate
1 dessertspoon honey
2 oz (50 g) butter

Butter two 8–8½ inch (20–21 cm) sandwich tins and line with discs of buttered greaseproof paper. Dust with flour. Either in a double boiler or in a bowl set over a pan of hot water, melt the chocolate until smooth. Remove from the heat and leave on one side to cool slightly. Whisk the butter until soft, then whisk in the sugar a bit at a time until light and fluffy. Whisk in the eggs one at a time, whisking well after each addition. The mixture may look curdled, but this does not matter. Heat the oven to Gas 5/375°F/190°C. Whisk the melted chocolate into the butter and egg mixture. On the lowest speed whisk in the ground hazelnuts and breadcrumbs, just until evenly mixed. Finally, stir in the grated orange rind. Spoon the mixture into the sandwich tins and smooth the tops. Bake in the centre of the oven for 20–25 minutes (this cake should not be overbaked), until the centre is firm to a very light touch.

Cool the cakes in the tins. Then loosen the edges with a knife and turn one cake carefully (as the cakes are delicate) on to a serving plate. Remove the greaseproof paper disc. Spread with a thin layer of marmalade. Then carefully turn the other cake on to a board, remove the greaseproof paper, and, with the help of a wide spatula, turn on to the other cake so that the top of the cake is uppermost. If necessary cut the edges of the cake to make it straight for icing.

To make the glaze simply put the chocolate, honey and butter in the top of a double boiler or in a bowl set over hot water and stir until melted and smooth. Replace the hot water underneath by very cold and stir the glaze until it thickens. Then pour it over the top of the cake and, using a spatula, spread the icing all down the sides of the cake too. Clean excess glaze from the plate with a damp paper towel. If liked, before the glaze is quite set, you can decorate the cake with toasted whole or chopped hazelnuts.

Henry's Chocolate Cake

Surely the best chocolate cakes are dark, moist, gooey and wickedly rich. They remain the favourite with both adults and children, and I first made this cake for my son's birthday. Covered with whipped cream and trickles of melted chocolate, it also makes an ideal pudding.

5 oz (150 g) plain chocolate
6 tablespoons water
4 oz (100 g) butter or margarine
4 oz (100 g) soft dark brown sugar
3 large eggs
2 oz (50 g) ground almonds

2 oz (50 g) fresh white bread, crusts removed
apricot jam
6 fl oz (175 ml) double or whipping cream

Butter a fairly shallow 7–8 inch (17·5–20 cm) cake tin and line with a disc of buttered greaseproof paper. Melt 4 oz (100 g) of the chocolate in the water and stir until smooth. Leave to cool slightly. Beat the butter until soft. Beat in the brown sugar until fluffy and then beat in the egg yolks, the ground almonds and the melted chocolate. Put the bread in a food processor and whizz until you have light breadcrumbs. Stir them into the chocolate mixture. Heat the oven to Gas 5/375°F/190°C. Whisk the egg whites until they stand in soft peaks, then, using a metal spoon, fold them gently into the chocolate mixture and spoon into the prepared cake tin. Bake in the centre of the oven for 40–50 minutes, until springy to a light touch in the centre. Cool in the tin.

When the cake is cold, loosen the edges with a knife and turn out. Melt the remaining 1 oz (25 g) of chocolate with 1 tablespoon of water. Stir until smooth and leave to cool. Put the cake on a serving plate and spread all over with apricot jam. Whisk the cream until thick, but not too stiff. Ice first the sides and then the top of the cake with the cream in rough flicks. Then, holding the spoon high above the cake, trickle the cooled chocolate over it in thin criss-cross patterns. Leave in a very cold place, but preferably not the fridge, until ready to serve.

Bitter Chocolate Cake

This is a luxurious combination of chocolate, ground nuts and eggs – dense, slightly gooey and iced with creamy bitter chocolate. It is perfect for a special occasion. I like it best served as a pudding, either with whipped cream slightly soured by gradually whisking in a little lemon juice or, best of all, with sharp lemon sorbet.

6 oz (175 g) dark plain chocolate
6 oz (175 g) butter or margarine
5 oz (150 g) caster sugar
6 large eggs, separated
6 oz (175 g) ground hazelnuts or almonds
pinch salt

For the icing
5 fl oz (150 ml) soured cream
2 teaspoons instant coffee
6–7 oz (175–200 g) dark plain chocolate, broken up

Decoration
chopped nuts or chocolate shavings

Butter a deep cake tin 9–10 inches (23–25 cm) by 2½–3 inches (6·5–7·5 cm), and line with a buttered disc of greaseproof paper. Dust with flour. Melt the chocolate either in a double saucepan or in a bowl over a pan of hot water, and set aside to cool slightly. Cream the butter and then beat in the caster sugar until light and fluffy. Add the egg yolks one at a time, beating them in thoroughly. Beat in the slightly cooled chocolate and then gradually beat in the ground nuts. Transfer the mixture to a large mixing bowl.

Heat the oven to Gas 6/400°F/200°C. Add a pinch of salt to the egg whites and whisk until they stand in soft peaks. Stir 2 tablespoons of hot water into the chocolate mixture to soften the consistency. Then stir in 1 heaped tablespoon of the whisked egg whites. In three batches, fold in the remaining egg whites with a spatula. Spoon into the prepared tin and smooth the top. Bake just below the centre of the pre-heated oven for 20 minutes, then reduce the heat to Gas 4/350°F/180°C and continue baking for another 40 minutes. (If using a 10 inch (25 cm) tin bake for only 35 minutes as the cake must not be overcooked – it must remain gooey in the centre.) Wet and wring out a tea towel, fold it in half and lay on a flat surface. Remove the cake from the oven and lay it, still in the tin, on the wet towel for about 20 minutes. Then carefully turn out, loosening the sides with a knife if necessary, on to a rack.

To make the icing, heat the soured cream over a gentle heat until just bubbling. Add the instant coffee and stir until dissolved. Add the broken-up chocolate. Stir over the heat for 1 minute, then remove and continue stirring until the chocolate is dissolved and smooth. Allow to cool for 10–15 minutes. (You can stick the pan in a bowl of cold water to speed up the cooling.) To make the icing easy and unmessy lay four strips (making a square) of greaseproof paper on a serving plate. Lay the cake on top so that the greaseproof sticks out all around it. Spoon the icing on top of the cake and then smooth it all over the top and round the sides. Decorate before it sets with chopped nuts or chocolate shavings.

Bitter Orange Cake (for 6–8)

A unique flavour is given to this cake by incorporating a purée of cooked whole oranges. It's a very moist cake with a slight crunchiness of almonds, and I think it is best of all served as a pudding, still slightly warm, with cream.

2 large or 3 small oranges	6 oz (175 g) plain flour
5 large eggs	1 teaspoon baking powder
salt	2 oz (50 g) flaked almonds
8 oz (225 g) soft brown sugar	icing sugar
2 oz (50 g) fine semolina	

Wash the oranges and put whole and unpeeled into a saucepan of water. Cover and boil for 2 hours, checking to make sure the water does not boil away. Then drain and let the oranges cool enough to cut open and remove any pips. Put them unpeeled into a liquidizer and whizz to a smooth purée. Butter and flour a deep 7½–8 inch (18·5–20 cm) cake tin, preferably one with a loose base. Whisk the eggs in a large bowl with a good pinch of salt until frothy, then whisk in the sugar, followed by the orange purée and the semolina. Then sift in the flour and baking powder and stir into the mixture. Gently stir in the almonds.

Heat the oven to Gas 4/350°F/180°C. Pour the mixture into the prepared cake tin and cook in the centre of the oven for 1–1¼ hours. (The top of the cake will probably look brown enough only half-way through the cooking – if so, lay a piece of greaseproof paper on top to stop it browning too much.) When cooked, let the cake cool in the tin for about 10 minutes or more. Then turn out on to a serving plate and sprinkle icing sugar through a sieve all over the top.

American Apple Cake (for 6–8)

If fudge did not mean something quite different – i.e. rich chocolate – in American cake recipes I would say this gungy pudding cake tasted like a sharp apple fudge. Anyway, it is bound to be popular.

5 oz (150 ml) plain flour
1 teaspoon baking powder
¼ teaspoon salt
2 level tablespoons caster sugar
2 oz (50 g) butter or margarine
1 large egg
½ teaspoon vanilla essence
milk

For the topping
approx. 1¼ lb (500 g) cooking apples
3 oz (75 g) butter or margarine
7 oz (200 g) light brown or demerara
  sugar
2 teaspoons ground cinnamon

Sift the flour, baking powder, salt and caster sugar into a mixing bowl. Cut in the 2 oz (50 g) butter and crumble with your fingertips, like making pastry, until the mixture is like fine breadcrumbs. In a measuring jug, whisk the egg and vanilla essence together and add enough milk to make up 4 fl oz (110 ml). Add to the flour and butter mixture and stir thoroughly. Spoon the batter into a buttered rectangular dish about 10 by 8 inches (25 by 20 cm). Heat the oven to Gas 7/425°F/220°C. Peel and slice the apples thinly and arrange them in closely overlapping rows on top of the batter. Melt the 3 oz (75 g) butter in a pan, stir in the brown sugar and cinnamon and spoon evenly over the apples. Bake in the centre of the oven for 25 minutes. Serve warm or cold with thin cream.

Frosted Lemon Egg Yolk Cake

This is a cake which it is sensible to make either before or after making meringues. It is an excellent cake, light in texture but rich in flavour and very easy to make.

3 oz (75 g) butter or margarine
6 oz (175 g) caster sugar
4 large egg yolks
1 large egg
7 oz (200 g) plain flour
2 teaspoons baking powder
¼ teaspoon salt
4 fl oz (110 ml) milk
finely grated rind of 1 lemon

For the frosting
1 large egg white
2 teaspoons plus ½ tablespoon lemon
  juice
8–9 oz (225–250 g) icing sugar, sifted

Décoration
a little candied peel or chopped nuts

Cream the butter and whisk in the caster sugar gradually until light and fluffy. Beat the egg yolks and the whole egg together and add a little at a time to the creamed butter and sugar, whisking thoroughly. Sift the flour, the baking powder and salt together and stir in, alternately with the milk. Stir in the lemon rind. Butter a 7 inch (17·5 cm) cake tin, line the bottom with a disc of buttered greaseproof paper and dust with flour. Heat the oven to Gas 4/350°F/180°C. Spoon the cake mixture into the tin and cook in the centre of the oven for 55–60 minutes until a sharp knife inserted in the centre comes out clean. Leave to cool in the tin and then loosen the sides if necessary and turn out right way up on to a rack for frosting.

Whisk the egg white until stiff, add the 2 teaspoons of lemon juice and whisk in the sifted icing sugar a bit at a time. Then whisk in the ½ tablespoon of lemon juice. (The frosting should have a thick spreading consistency – if necessary, whisk in a little more icing sugar.) Using a wide knife or spatula, spread the frosting all over the cake in rough flicks. Sprinkle a little candied peel or chopped nuts on top and leave to let the frosting set for several hours, overnight if you like.

Sultana Curd Cake

This is an excellent type of cheesecake, more like the continental kind but still light and less sickly than the American cheesecake can be. You can serve it either as a cake for tea or as a pudding, with thin cream.

For the pastry
6 oz (175 g) plain flour
4 oz (100 g) butter
2 tablespoons cold water

For the filling
2 oz (50 g) butter
8 oz (225 g) curd cheese

2 oz (50 g) caster sugar
1½ oz (40 g) self-raising flour
2 tablespoons cream or top of the milk
3 eggs, separated
large handful sultanas
pinch cream of tartar

Make the pastry in the usual way. Grease a deep 6–7 inch (15–17·5 cm) loose-bottomed cake tin. Roll out the pastry into a circle 1–2 inches (2·5–5 cm) bigger than the diameter of the tin. Place the circle of pastry in the tin, pressing it up the sides – it doesn't matter at all if the edge is uneven. Put the tin in the fridge while you prepare the filling.

Cream the butter with the curd cheese until soft, add the sugar and whisk until light. Sift in the flour, and add the cream and the egg yolks. Whizz all together thoroughly until soft and smooth and stir in the sultanas. Heat the oven to Gas 5/375°F/190°C. Add the cream of tartar to the egg whites, whisk until they stand in peaks and, using a metal spoon, fold lightly into the cheese mixture. Pour into the pastry-lined tin and bake in the centre of the oven for 40–50 minutes until well risen, and when a small knife inserted in the centre comes out clean. (Towards the end of the cooking you can place a piece of brown paper or foil on top of the cake if it is getting too brown.) Leave the cake in the tin until cold (it may sink slightly but this does not matter) and then loosen the edges with a knife and push out.

Sally Lunn Cake

This is one of the best and most famous enriched tea breads. It has a very light texture, golden and glazed on top and pale beneath. I like to put in plenty of lemon and orange rind, which smells lovely while it is cooking.

½ oz (15 g) fresh yeast
1 teaspoon sugar
a little warm milk
10 oz (275 g) strong white bread flour
1 teaspoon salt
grated rind of 1 large lemon and 1
  orange

1 teaspoon mixed spice
4 fl oz (110 ml) cream
2 eggs, beaten
1 dessertspoon sugar
1 dessertspoon milk

Put the yeast into a large cup with the sugar and a little warm milk to cover. Leave on one side. Sift the flour and salt into a bowl, and add the grated rinds, spice, cream, yeast liquid and beaten eggs. Beat to a thickish batter, thick enough to form lightly into a round shape, using well-floured hands (if it seems very slack add a little more flour). Put the dough into a deep greased 6 inch (15 cm) cake tin, put into a loose polythene bag and leave in a fairly warm place until risen to the top of the tin. Heat the oven to Gas 6/400°F/200°C and bake in the centre of the oven for 15 minutes.

While the cake is hot in the tin, boil the sugar and milk up together and brush this glaze over the top of the cake. When the cake is cool enough, loosen the sides carefully with a knife and turn out. It is best eaten still warm and spread with butter.

The Best Christmas Pudding

So named because it simply is the best Christmas pudding I have eaten. As it has no sugar and no flour it is lighter in texture than usual, and much more palatable after a rich meal. Everyone always seems to have a second helping and there is hardly ever any left over. I have a very sweet tooth but the large amount of dried fruit sweetens the pudding perfectly well. This quantity will fill one 2 pint (1·1 litre) pudding basin and probably a small basin as well. (If you want a completely round pudding, which has such an old-fashioned Dickensian appearance, buy yourself a round Chinese rice steamer. Line it with foil and fill each side with the mixture before fastening together and cooking for a bit longer than usual to get it nice and dark all through.)

3 oz (75 g) glacé cherries
6 oz (175 g) candied peel
12 oz (350 g) seedless raisins
6 oz (175 g) sultanas

6 oz (175 g) currants
3 oz (75 g) split almonds
8 oz (225 g) fresh white breadcrumbs
8 oz (225 g) shredded suet

1 teaspoon ground cinnamon
¼ whole nutmeg, grated
6 eggs

¼ pint (150 ml) Guinness
3 tablespoons brandy, rum or whisky

Generously butter the pudding basins or the foil lining of the rice steamer. Chop up the glacé cherries roughly. Put the dried fruit, almonds, breadcrumbs, suet and spices into a large bowl and mix thoroughly. Whisk the eggs until frothy and stir into the dry ingredients. Lastly stir in the beer and brandy, enough to make a mixture which just drops from the spoon. Spoon the mixture into the pudding basins, almost filling them up, and smooth the tops. Cover with a double layer of well-buttered foil and tie tightly round with string, making a string handle for lifting the basins out.

Put the basins, preferably on a rack or inverted saucer, into a large and smaller saucepan and pour in boiling water to come three-quarters of the way up the sides of the basins. Cover the pans and steam for about 6–7 hours for the larger basin and 3–4 hours for the smaller basin, checking to see if the water needs topping up after about 2 hours. When the puddings are cold put them away in a dark cool place, where they will keep for 2 or 3 months if necessary.

On Christmas Day replace the buttered foil with clean layers and steam for another hour or so before serving with brandy butter or whipped cream, (If using the rice steamer, you can take the pudding out when it has cooled a bit and store it wrapped in foil, then put it back in the steamer for re-cooking on Christmas Day.)

Golden Christmas Cake

This cake is much lighter than a traditional Christmas cake. It is made with paler fruits and walnuts and has a refreshing sharp flavour which I think is a very good contrast to the Christmas pudding.

6 oz (175 g) dried apricots
1 rounded tablespoon thick or 2
 tablespoons clear honey
5 tablespoons brandy or sherry
8 oz (225 g) glacé cherries
2 oz (50 g) angelica
4 oz (100 g) crystallized ginger
4 oz (100 g) crystallized pineapple

8 oz (225 g) butter, plus extra for
 greasing
grated rind and juice of 1 lemon
8 oz (225 g) caster sugar
4 oz (100 g) ground almonds
4 eggs
4 oz (100 g) plain flour
½ teaspoon salt
4 oz (100 g) chopped walnuts

Cut up the dried apricots roughly and put into a bowl. Dissolve the honey in the brandy or sherry over a low heat and pour on to the apricots. Leave to soak for several hours. Butter an 8 inch (20 cm) cake tin and line the base with 2 discs of buttered greaseproof paper. Press a piece of double foil round the outside of the tin, to come up 1–2 inches (2·5–5 cm) above the rim for protection. Roughly chop the glacé cherries, angelica, ginger and pineapple. Whisk the butter with the grated lemon rind until soft and then whisk in the caster sugar until light and fluffy. Add the ground almonds. In another bowl beat the eggs thoroughly until they have increased in volume and are pale and thickened. Add the beaten eggs to the cake mixture a little at a time, whisking well after each addition. Sift in the flour and salt and stir in lightly with a metal spoon. Then stir in the lemon juice. Add the chopped dried fruits, the walnut pieces and finally the soaked apricots and their juices.

Heat the oven to Gas 4/350°F/180°C. The cake mixture should just drop from the spoon with a good shake – if it does not, add a little more brandy. Spoon the mixture into the prepared tin, smooth the top and make an even depression in the centre. Bake for 1½ hours and then turn down the heat to Gas 1/275°F/140°C, and after another 20–30 minutes lay a piece of foil on top of the cake so that it doesn't get any browner. Continue cooking for another 2 hours. Let the cake cool in the tin, then loosen the sides with a knife and turn out. Wrap thoroughly in greaseproof paper and then foil and store in a cool place.

I simply ice this cake with fluffy American frosting, which looks so very snow-like, the day before we eat it. But if you prefer you can use the traditional marzipan and royal icing instead.

Casablanca Cakes

Extremely quick and easy, these are a good thing for children to make when they are starting to cook. They are half cake, half biscuit, crunchy yet gooey, with the flavours of almond and lemon. Very useful as an accompaniment to ice creams, fruit fools or compôtes.

1 large egg
4 oz (100 g) icing sugar
½ teaspoon baking powder
2 oz (50 g) ground almonds

4 oz (100 g) fine semolina
finely grated rind of 1 lemon
extra icing sugar

Whisk the egg with the icing sugar until very pale. Stir in the baking powder, ground almonds, semolina and lemon rind. Mix thoroughly together. Heat the oven to Gas 4/350°F/180°C. Grease a large baking sheet and put out a small bowl of sifted icing sugar. Wet your hands with water, take up pieces of the mixture and form into balls the size of large marbles, dipping one side of each ball in the icing sugar and then placing the balls on the baking sheet sugar side up and very well spaced out as they spread quite a bit. You will probably have to cook the cakes in two batches. Bake in the centre of the oven for 10–12 minutes until very pale brown. Ease the biscuits off the baking sheet carefully with a palette knife and cool on a rack.

Honey and Orange Wholemeal Biscuits

These are easy to make and have a very good flavour.

4 oz (100 g) soft margarine
2 oz (50 g) soft light brown sugar
1 rounded tablespoon honey

5 oz (150 g) wholemeal flour
finely grated rind of 1 orange

Heat the oven to Gas 5/375°F/190°C. Grease a large baking tray. Whisk or beat the margarine, sugar and honey until light and fluffy. Stir in the flour and orange rind and mix thoroughly. Drop teaspoons of the mixture on to the prepared tray, and bake just above the centre of the oven for 10–15 minutes until golden brown and firm. Remove the biscuits with a spatula and cool on a wire rack.

Cheese and Tomato Thins

Featherlight savoury biscuits fitting for any occasion, and made in the convenient 'ice-box' way which enables you to have freshly baked biscuits within 10 minutes at any time.

4 oz (100 g) plain flour
1 teaspoon baking powder
½ teaspoon salt
1 teaspoon caster sugar

3 oz (75 g) butter
2 oz (50 g) grated cheese
1 tablespoon tomato purée
grated Parmesan cheese (optional)

Sift the flour, baking powder, salt and caster sugar into a bowl. Rub in the butter until crumbly, mix in the grated cheese and the tomato purée thoroughly (or do all this within seconds in a food processor). Using floured hands, gather up the dough and form into a long roll about 1½ inches (3·5 cm) in diameter. Wrap the roll up in cling film and place carefully on a flat surface in the freezing compartment of the fridge. When frozen, heat the oven to Gas 4/350°F/180°C, slice off rounds as thinly as possible and place fairly close together on a large baking sheet. (Put the remainder of the roll back in the freezer.) Sprinkle the biscuits with a little grated Parmesan and bake in the centre of the oven for 7–8 minutes. Ease the biscuits off the baking sheet with a palette knife while still warm, and cool on a rack. (Make another batch of biscuits from the frozen roll if you want them, or leave it for another occasion.)

Walnut and Peel Biscuits

Light and tempting little biscuits, suitable for any occasion and particularly good with ice cream. The dough is frozen in the convenient 'American ice-box' way which enables you to have freshly baked biscuits within 10 minutes whenever you want them. (If you have a food processor you can simply mix all the ingredients up in it together, which makes this recipe truly effortless.)

4 oz (100 g) butter	2 oz (50 g) candied peel, finely chopped
7 oz (200 g) soft pale brown sugar	7 oz (200 g) plain flour
1 large egg	2 teaspoons baking powder
2 oz (50 g) walnuts, finely chopped	¼ teaspoon salt

Cream the butter and sugar together until soft. Beat or whisk in the egg thoroughly. Mix in the chopped walnuts and peel. Then sift in the flour, baking powder and salt and mix into the dough with a wooden spoon. Spoon the dough on to a sheet of greaseproof paper, roll the paper over, and shape the dough by moulding it into a round or oblong shape about 12–14 inches (30–35 cm) long. Put this roll on a baking sheet and freeze in the freezing compartment of the fridge or a freezer for 30 minutes or more.

To bake, heat the oven to Gas 7/425°F/220°C. Take out the frozen dough, peel off the greaseproof paper and lay the roll on a board. Using a very sharp knife, cut across very thinly into roundish biscuits. Lay these ¾ inch (1·5 cm) apart on a baking sheet. Bake the biscuits towards the top of the oven for 7–9 minutes until mid brown. Remove the biscuits carefully with a spatula while still hot and leave to cool. Continue in batches until you have as many biscuits as you need, putting the remaining dough back in the freezer for another time.

Walnut Brownie Thins

I find these more irresistible than American brownies. They have the same rich chocolate and nut flavour but are thin and light. They are also even easier to make. They have a crisp top with a slightly gooey underneath which is how I like them – if you want to make them more firmly crisp, cook them for a further 5 minutes.

4 oz (100 g) butter or margarine
1 oz (25 g) dark bitter chocolate
1 teaspoon instant coffee
3 oz (75 g) soft dark brown sugar
½ teaspoon vanilla essence

1 egg, whisked
1 oz (25 g) plain flour
½ teaspoon salt
2 oz (50 g) shelled walnuts, roughly chopped

Butter a Swiss roll tin about 10 by 14 inches (25 by 35 cm), and heat the oven to Gas 5/375°F/190°C. In a heavy saucepan melt the butter and chocolate over the lowest heat. Stir with a wooden spoon until smooth. Add the instant coffee and stir to dissolve. Remove from the heat and stir in the sugar and vanilla essence. Add the whisked egg and mix thoroughly. Sift in the flour and salt and mix until smooth. Pour into the prepared tin and spread evenly. Sprinkle all over with the chopped walnuts. Bake below the centre of the oven for 15 minutes, turning the tin round half-way through the cooking to ensure even browning. Remove from the oven and cut at once, carefully, with a sharp knife, into squares or oblongs. Then remove the biscuits with a metal spatula while still warm and cool on a rack.

American Buttermilk Griddle Cakes

My children adore pancakes, but they do take a long time to make – I seem to stand at the stove for hours and everyone eats them up as fast as I cook them so there are never any left for me. These griddle cakes are a quick and easy alternative, similar to Scotch pancakes but nutritiously made with buttermilk and with a slight crunch to them which people like. Serve them either as a pudding while they are still hot, with maple or golden syrup, melted butter and even cream too, or simply cold for tea, spread with butter and jam or honey.

9 fl oz (250 ml) buttermilk	1 tablespoon melted butter
3 fl oz (90 ml) milk	1 oz (25 g) cornmeal or semolina
1 large egg, whisked	8 oz (225 g) plain flour, sifted
1 level teaspoon bicarbonate of soda	butter to grease pan
1 level teaspoon salt	

Mix the first 8 ingredients together in the order given and stir or whisk until smooth. Heat a griddle or a large, heavy frying pan to a medium heat. Melt a knob of butter to grease the surface. Drop in tablespoons of the batter a little apart and cook on one side until they are puffed up and bubbles are rising. Turn with a spatula and cook briefly until golden brown on the other side. Transfer the cooked griddle cakes to a plate and continue with the batter until it is used up, adding butter to grease the pan as necessary and turning down the heat if they brown too much.

Apricot Whirls

Wonderfully impressive tricks can be done with bought puff pastry. These crisp, delicate little patisseries are so easy to make, yet they could well have been bought in France. They go well as an accompaniment to fruit fools and ice cream, or just to nibble with coffee or tea.

8 oz (225 g) packet puff pastry
2–3 tablespoons caster sugar
apricot jam

Roll out the pastry on a floured board into a rectangle measuring about 13 by 10 inches (32·5 by 25 cm). Sprinkle evenly all over with the caster sugar. Heat the oven to Gas 7/425°F/220°C. Roll up the piece of pastry somewhat loosely starting from the longer side. (If you want larger whirls roll up from the shorter side.) Moisten the edge and press lightly down to secure. Using a sharp knife, cut across the roll into ⅓ inch (8 mm) wide whirls. Lay them, spaced a little apart, on a large, damp baking sheet. Bake towards the top of the oven for 10–12 minutes until light golden brown. Turn the whirls over and bake for another 4–5 minutes. Remove at once from the tray with a spatula and spread with apricot jam while still hot. Leave to cool.

Golden Puffs

These are little circles of orange and lemon flavoured dough which puff up when deep fried in oil. Children love them. Use groundnut oil if possible, as it has little taste or smell.

1 lb (450 g) self-raising flour
grated peel of 1 large orange and 1 lemon
2 eggs, whisked

4 oz (100 g) melted butter
milk
caster sugar
lemon wedges

Sift the flour into a bowl. Add the orange and the lemon peel. Stir in the whisked eggs, the melted butter and enough milk to bind. Beat, using an electric dough hook if you have one, until you have a smooth, thick dough. Cover the bowl with plastic film or foil and refrigerate for at least 1 hour. Then knead the dough a little on a well-floured board and roll out as thinly as possible. Cut rounds with a fluted biscuit cutter and fry them in medium to hot oil until well puffed up and pale golden brown. Pile up on a plate, sprinkle with plenty of caster sugar, and serve with lemon wedges.

Molasses Bread

This is so quick and easy to make for tea. Vary it by using honey or golden syrup instead of the molasses. It is best eaten sliced and buttered.

6 oz (175 g) plain flour
1 teaspoon bicarbonate of soda
½ teaspoon cream of tartar
good pinch salt
2 oz (50 g) butter or margarine

1 tablespoon caster sugar
1 tablespoon molasses
1 egg, beaten
4–5 tablespoon milk

Heat the oven to Gas 3/325°F/170°C. Sift the flour, bicarbonate of soda, cream of tartar and salt into a bowl. Rub in the butter. Stir in the sugar, molasses, beaten egg and milk. Mix well with a wooden spoon to a dropping consistency, adding a little more milk if necessary. Spoon into a small greased loaf tin (the mixture should only half fill the tin as it rises a lot). Bake in the centre of the oven for 40–50 minutes, until well risen and firm to touch. For an appetizing sheen brush with ½ tablespoon of caster sugar dissolved in a tablespoon of hot water immediately on removing from the oven. Cool in the tin.

Bitty Brown Bread

This is a fairly dense nutty-flavoured bread full of roughage and excellent with cold salad meals and cheese or simply for tea with plenty of honey.

1 lb (450 g) wholemeal flour
1 lb (450 g) strong white flour
4 oz (100 g) whole wheat grains
2 oz (50 g) bran
2 oz (50 g) sesame seeds
1 level tablespoon sea salt, crushed
½ teaspoon ground mace

¾ oz (20 g) fresh yeast (or under
½ oz (15 g) dried yeast)
2 fl oz (50 ml) sunflower oil
1 level tablespoon soft brown sugar
about ¾ pint (450 ml) lukewarm
water

Put the flour, grains, bran, sesame seeds, salt and mace into a bowl. Cover it and put in a very low oven for about 5–10 minutes until the flour is warm. Meanwhile put the yeast in a cup and just cover with tepid water (if using dried yeast, add water a pinch of sugar and leave for 10 minutes for it to come back to active life). Put the oil, sugar and lukewarm water into a warm jug together.

Take the flour from the oven. Pour the creamed yeast into the centre, then stir it in with a wooden spoon, adding the liquid from the jug gradually. Work with your hands for 2 or 3 minutes until the dough comes away easily from the sides of the bowl. Sprinkle on more flour if it seems sticky. Form into a ball, sprinkle with flour and cover the bowl with polythene. Leave in a fairly warm place for 1½–2 hours until the dough has doubled in size. Knock it back with a fierce punch and slap it hard against the bowl several times. Then knead it on a floured surface for about 5 minutes, spreading it out and folding it over again roughly. Divide the dough into two equal pieces and shape into two loaves with the fold at the bottom. Put into two warmed greased medium-sized bread tins. Cover with polythene and leave in a warm place for 45–60 minutes until well risen.

Brush the top of the bread with warm water and sprinkle over some extra sesame seeds. Bake in the centre of the oven at Gas 7/425°F/220°C for 20 minutes, then at Gas 5/375°F/190°C for another 25–35 minutes until the bread sounds hollow when tapped underneath. Cool on a wire rack.

Cheese and Onion Bread

This rich bread is a perfect accompaniment to a light meal of cold meat, particularly salami, and salad. Try to eat the bread either still warm or re-heated in the oven.

1 oz (25 g) fresh yeast or ½ oz (15 g) dried	3 teaspoons mustard powder
6 fl oz (175 ml) warm, not hot, milk	8 oz (225 g) strong cheese, grated
3 oz (75 g) butter or margarine	8 oz (225 g) onions, finely chopped
6 oz (175 g) strong white bread flour	2 eggs, beaten
14 oz (400 g) wholemeal flour	2–4 teaspoons salt (sea salt is best)
	a little extra grated cheese

Put the yeast into a bowl with 2 teaspoons of sugar. Add the milk, stir, and leave on one side for about 10 minutes. Rub the butter into the mixed flours and mustard powder. Add the cheese, onions, beaten eggs, salt and the yeast liquid. Mix thoroughly with a wooden spoon. Using floured hands, as it will be a soft, sticky dough, knead lightly on a floured surface until smooth. Divide the dough in half and put into two greased bread tins. Using a sharp knife, cut 3 or 4 slanting slits on top of the loaves. Put into a large polythene bag and leave in a warm place until doubled in size. Heat the oven to Gas 6/400°F/200°C. Sprinkle a little extra cheese on top of the loaves and bake in the centre of the oven for 45 minutes.

Soda Baps with Cheese and Leek

(makes 6 baps)

These are always welcome for quick lunches, children's suppers and picnics. Cheese and leeks are sandwiched between the raw dough and then cooked with it so that they ooze tantalizingly out of the sides. You can experiment with all sorts of fillings; sliced cooked chicken, mushrooms and garlic, or chopped ham, tomatoes and cheese with oregano. These are all popular in our family.

For the baps
1 lb (450 g) wholemeal flour *or* 8 oz
 (225 g) wholemeal flour and 8 oz
 (225 g) strong white flour
2 level teaspoons bicarbonate of
 soda
2 level teaspoons cream of tartar
1 teaspoon salt

½ pint milk (300 ml) soured with the
 juice of 1 lemon *or* ½ pint (300 ml)
 buttermilk

For the filling
butter
1 medium-sized leek, finely chopped
4 oz (100 g) cheese, grated
salt, black pepper

Mix the flour, bicarbonate of soda, cream of tartar and salt in a bowl. Stir in the soured milk and mix well until the dough leaves the sides of the bowl. Heat the oven to Gas 6/400°F/200°C. Gather up the dough and knead lightly on a floured board. Form into a longish roll and cut into 12 equal pieces. Roll out a little to form thickish flat circles about 4 inches (10 cm) in diameter. Lay 6 circles on a large greased baking sheet and dot them with butter. Then sprinkle on the chopped leek and grated cheese. Dot again with butter and season with salt and pepper. Top with the remaining circles of dough, press down round the edges, and brush with softened butter or oil. Bake in the centre of the oven for 20–25 minutes. Eat warm.

Syrian Picnic Breads (for 5–6)

One of the things I find most evocative of my childhood in the Middle East is the flavour of lamb mingled with cumin and fresh mint, which we used to eat stuffed into flat unleavened bread on our picnics in the cool hills above Damascus. Using Greek pitta bread it is possible to do the same sort of thing here. If you like the stuffed breads to stay warm for your picnic, wrap each one in foil and then in layers of newspaper. They make one of those complete meals that are so useful for outdoor eating.

6 pitta breads
1 oz (25 g) butter or margarine
1 lb (450 g) lamb or beef mince
2–3 cloves garlic, finely chopped
2 teaspoons ground cumin

12 oz (350 g) tomatoes, roughly sliced
small handful fresh mint leaves, chopped
1 small cos lettuce, sliced in shreds
salt, black pepper

Wrap the pitta breads in foil and put in a low oven to warm up. Heat the butter or margarine in a large frying pan. Add the mince and stir and break it up over a fairly high heat for about 5 minutes, until brown. Then stir in the garlic and cumin. Lower the heat and add the sliced tomatoes. Continue cooking fairly gently, stirring often, until the tomatoes are completely soft and the juices have evaporated. Season to taste with salt and black pepper, remove from the heat and stir in the mint and lettuce. Using a sharp knife, cut through the pitta breads down the side making a pocket, and stuff the mixture into them.

Index

MORE ABOUT PENGUINS, PELICANS AND PUFFINS

For further information about books available from Penguins please write to Dept EP, Penguin Books Ltd, Harmondsworth, Middlesex UB7 0DA.

In the U.S.A.: For a complete list of books available from Penguins in the United States write to Dept D G, Penguin Books, 299 Murray Hill Parkway, East Rutherford, New Jersey 07073.

In Canada: For a complete list of books available from Penguins in Canada write to Penguin Books Canada Ltd, 2801 John Street, Markham, Ontario L3R 1B4.

In Australia: For a complete list of books available from Penguins in Australia write to the Marketing Department, Penguin Books Australia Ltd, P.O. Box 257, Ringwood, Victoria 3134.

In New Zealand: For a complete list of books available from Penguins in New Zealand write to the Marketing Department, Penguin Books (N.Z.) Ltd, P.O. Box 4019, Auckland 10.

In India: For a complete list of books available from Penguins in India write to Penguin Overseas Ltd, 706 Eros Apartments, 56 Nehru Place, New Delhi 110019.

JOSCELINE DIMBLEBY'S BOOK OF PUDDINGS, DESSERTS AND SAVOURIES

Puddings to make the family gasp, desserts to amaze a formal gathering, savouries to round off a perfect meal . . .

Here Josceline Dimbleby has gathered together a selection of pies, tarts, gâteaux, mousses, cheesecakes, ice-creams and savouries which will inspire even the most jaded cook. Practical, easy and often inspired by the flavours of the Orient, they can be relied on to add a new dimension to your cooking.

GERALDENE HOLT'S CAKE STALL

Honey Crunch Tea-Bread, Praline Cream Gâteau, Harvest Cake, Iced Gingerbread, Chocolate Cup Cakes, Easter Biscuits.

These are only a selection of the delicious wares that Geraldene Holt sold from her enormously successful cake stall at Tiverton Pannier Market. (Now there are a string of similar cake stalls all over the country.) Collected into this book, her recipes will tempt even the most hard-hearted into action, and her advice on equipment, techniques and useful short cuts to success will ensure that hungry families everywhere are treated to amazing tea-time delights.

MEDITERRANEAN COOKBOOK
Arabella Boxer

Politically and linguistically diverse as they may be, the countries of the Mediterranean do share many culinary features in common. Arabella Boxer's meticulously researched and beautifully put together book constitutes a gastronomic grand tour of a region where spices, olives, tomatoes, yoghurt, salads, fruit and clever use of fish and meat combine so satisfyingly and memorably.

'Arabella Boxer has managed to conjure up the rich and colourful atmosphere of Mediterranean food ... a great resource for cooks and a solid piece of work on the real conditions in which these recipes first took root and flourished' – *Sunday Times*

SIMPLE FRENCH FOOD
Richard Olney

With recipes for pâtés and hearty soups, vegetable gratins, fish, meat and poultry, salads and desserts, *Simple French Food* became a cookery cult, and is now a classic. Here Richard Olney gives us inventive, gourmet variations on scrambled eggs, mouth-watering ways with aubergines, a bread pudding with kirsch and pistachios ... plus detailed instructions on preparing meat, a section on herbs and helpful information on bread, cheeses and wine in cooking.

'I have never read a book on French cuisine that has so excited and absorbed me' – Simone Beck, co-author of *Mastering the Art of French Cooking*